LIVING WITH DYSPRAXIA

A Guide for Adults with Developmental Dyspraxia

Revised Edition

Mary Colley

Foreword by Victoria Biggs
Introduction by Amanda Kirby

Jessica Kingsley Publishers
London and Philadelphia

First published in 2000 by the Dyspraxia Foundation Adult Support Group.

Revised third edition published in 2005 by DANDA: Developmental Adult Neuro-Diversity Association.

This edition published in 2006 by
Jessica Kingsley Publishers
116 Pentonville Road
London N1 9JB, UK
and
400 Market Street, Suite 400
Philadelphia, PA 19106, USA

www.jkp.com

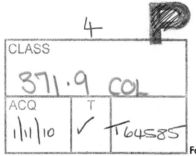

Library of Congress Cataloging in Publication Data

Colley, Mary.
Living with dyspraxia : a guide for adults with developmental
dyspraxia / Mary Colley ; foreword by Victoria Biggs. -- Rev. ed.
p. cm.
Includes bibliographical references (p.) and index.
ISBN-13: 978-1-84310-452-0 (pbk. : alk. paper)
ISBN-10: 1-84310-452-0 (pbk. : alk. paper)
1. Apraxia--Popular works. I. Title.
RC394.A75C65 2006
616.85'52--dc22

2006019757

British Library Cataloguing in Publication Data
A CIP catalogue record for this book is available from the British Library

ISBN 978 1 84310 452 0

Printed and bound in Great Britain by
MGP Books Group

CONTENTS

FOREWORD

Once known as 'clumsy child syndrome', developmental dyspraxia used to be perceived as a disorder from Neverland – a childhood problem that vanishes with age. Even now, the majority of books about dyspraxia focus on primary-school-aged children and are written specifically for parents and teachers. *Living with Dyspraxia* is the first book to openly challenge the Neverland myth, a myth that has caused countless adults to enter the world of work with their special needs unrecognised and unmet.

This book is a treasure trove of excellent advice. It includes coping strategies on topics as diverse as cookery, learning to drive, studying at university, and applying for a job. Mary has also done her readers a great favour by acknowledging the significant overlap between dyspraxia, the autistic spectrum and the other specific learning differences. For most people, dyspraxia is much more than a co-ordination disorder – a fact that sometimes goes unrecognised.

I have been greatly helped by this book. My own copy is well thumbed and streaked with orange highlighter. Practical, concise, and devoid of self-pity, *Living with Dyspraxia* fills a gap on the bookshelves that has stood empty for much too long.

Recently I was talking to a 21-year-old woman about her experiences in education. She has a cocktail of learning differences, including dyspraxia, dyslexia, auditory processing difficulties and autism. She was unable to speak until she was nine years old and the true nature of her difficulties was only discovered when she was 19. Now she is at university, studying to become an educational psychologist. Despite the unsympathetic and often downright abusive treatment she received as a child with hidden disabilities, she has retained a hopeful and gentle approach to life – an approach that the people who know her can only wonder at.

Sadly, there is a tendency for adults who were failed by the educational and medical systems to become very angry when they finally receive a diagnosis. If you are someone who is only just coming to terms with dyspraxia, it must be realised that this book does not set out the terms of your death sentence. It is a fresh expression of DANDA's philosophy on the role of neuro-divergent people – 'Nothing about us without us' – and offers its readers the support and information they need to live with dyspraxia. Not against it, not in spite of it, but with it.

Victoria Biggs, author of Caged in Chaos

ACKNOWLEDGEMENTS

Writing this book has not been easy. However, considering the number of people that have been involved and the fact that most of them are dyspraxic, I don't think we've done a bad job!

My thanks are due to many people. First to Sylvia Paul and her family, without whom the book would not have been possible. Jenny Peterson copyedited the book and kept me in order (not an easy task!). She made sure that I did not make the book even longer and translated my dyspraxic English into something much more readable.

I would also like to thank Dorothy Penso, a paediatric occupational therapist who has a great interest in adults with dyspraxia, and who has the condition mildly. She helped a great deal in the writing of the communication, relaxation and organisation chapters. I am also grateful to Colin Revell who helped with the chapters on definitions, assessment and independent living in particular, and to Paul Gardner who did most of the work on the case studies. Thank you also to Dr Amanda Kirby, who helped so much by finding time in her phenomenally busy schedule to advise on the book and write the introduction. I am particularly grateful to Diana Bartlett who helped me with this edition of the book.

Thanks go also to the many other contributors to the book; in particular, Diana Bartlett, Andrew Burniston, Judith Campbell, Caroline Hands, Jonathan Garland, Eleanor Howes, David Hunt, Melanie Jameson, Penny Stafford, Jo Todd, Dianne Zaccheo and Barbara Zanditon. I am also very grateful to my family.

Last but not least, thank you to all those individuals with dyspraxia, from all over the world, who have shared their experiences of having dyspraxia with me and others and asked so many of the questions that I have tried to answer in the book. Without them, the book would not have been possible.

INTRODUCTION

This book has been written for those adults who wonder why they find some things in their lives so much harder than other people. It provides a commonsense approach to many of the problems that individuals with co-ordination difficulties face on a day-to-day basis.

The information in the book can give other people some insight into what life with co-ordination difficulties is like. It may give medical professionals, social workers, colleges' special needs teachers and careers officers ideas for helping adults with the condition. Employers might use the information to assist the adults to integrate into the workplace more fully.

Professionals who work with children now have better understanding of dyspraxia and related conditions. Over the past few years services for this group have started to appear across the UK.

However we sometimes forget that the children grow into adults, and that those adults may still require some help and support to be able to have a fulfilled and happy life. At present there are few opportunities for help for the individuals who have problems. Their difficulties may affect their ability to do certain tasks; and may also impact on their skills to make and maintain relationships. This can have a deleterious effect when trying to get and keep a job, or to meet people and have a successful relationship.

Some adults with co-ordination difficulties feel very despondent and even become depressed. Finding appropriate help can be a long and tiring job. There are few services set up to help the adult who doesn't fit into the remit of either the mental health services or the learning disability services. For many people it means 'falling through the gap' and just accepting whatever help is available in their area, whether or not that help meets their specific needs.

Adults with dyspraxia may face the challenge of gaining employment. They may be thwarted even before they get to the interview. Their handwriting may be poor and their interview skills erratic. Many of the skills required to improve employability are pinpointed in this book, and should help individuals to gain the confidence to be more successful.

Mary Colley has worked tirelessly to produce this book along with her contributors, many of whom have experienced the problems and come up with solutions. They express their views and give their ideas and tips on how to make other people's lives easier and less stressful.

So often we try to find a label to solve the problems, rather than help to find solutions to the problems themselves. This book considers the problems of dyspraxia and applies practical solutions. It is not a diagnostic book. It is not a scientific book, but a practical self-help guide to common problems with many useful and well-tested ideas. Adults who may not have co-ordination difficulties but who wish to become more organised and able in both the home and the workplace could benefit from reading it.

DANDA (the Developmental Adult Neuro-Diversity Association) and the Dyspraxia Foundation's Adult Support Group have helped many adults over the past few years. The Group represents adults, some of whom are only now recognising that as children they experienced problems. The Group provides a network of support and tries to ensure that there is wider understanding of the difficulties faced by adults with this specific learning difficulty.

If we can identify at an early stage those individuals who have dyspraxia, there is a greater chance that as adults many of their problems can be minimised. This book shows that even if there are problems later on there are many constructive ideas that can make life more satisfying and fulfilling.

Many thanks must go to Mary and all the contributors to this book. Mary has pushed and cajoled everyone in the nicest way to make this possible. If it wasn't for her enthusiasm, then it would not have happened.

Amanda Kirby, The Dyscovery Centre,
author of The Adolescent with Developmental
Co-ordination Disorder (DCD)

How to use this book

This is a reference book – just dip into it using the index at the back.

 Wherever you see this symbol you will find suggestions for further reading.

 Look for this symbol if you need more information and contact addresses.

Chapter 1

WHAT IS DEVELOPMENTAL DYSPRAXIA?

A definition of dyspraxia

Dyspraxia is a delay or disorder of the planning and/or execution of complex movements. It may be developmental – part of an individual's make up – or it can be acquired at any stage in life as the result of brain illness or injury as in a stroke. Associated with this may be problems of language, perception and thought.

There is frequently an overlap between dyspraxia and other developmental problems. Some people have developmental speech and language problems and may grow to have a mixture of dyslexia and co-ordination problems. In the experience of DANDA, attention deficit disorder (known as ADD or ADHD) and hyperactivity are also often associated with the condition as well as Asperger's syndrome and Tourette's syndrome. (Of course, some dyspraxic people exhibit only dyspraxic symptoms, but the majority experience an overlap with other developmental conditions; see neuro-diversity diagram p.161.)

Most people with dyspraxia are of normal intelligence, though there is an increased risk of global learning difficulties for people with the condition.

Other terms for developmental dyspraxia include develop-mental co-ordination disorder (DCD), motor learning difficulties, motor dysfunction, perceptuo-motor difficulties, and DAMP (disorder of attention, motor control and perception). The terms 'clumsy child syndrome' and 'minimal brain damage' are now fortunately obsolete.

What causes dyspraxia?

There is no known cause for the condition, although it is thought to be an immaturity of neurone development in the brain rather than brain damage. Our understanding of the causes of dyspraxia may change as medical research progresses.

Who is affected by dyspraxia?

Most people with dyspraxia are of normal intelligence

Dyspraxia is thought to affect up to 10 per cent of the population and up to 4 per cent severely. Dyspraxia can be an inherited condition.

What are the symptoms of dyspraxia?

People with impaired co-ordination and/or perception often have great difficulties in performing routine tasks such as driving, household chores, cooking and grooming themselves. (While those with the most severe dyspraxia will have all these symptoms, most will have more than their fair share of co-ordination and perceptual difficulties. Those with milder dyspraxia may exhibit only a few symptoms. They may wish to highlight those symptoms that apply to them before showing the list to others.) Many dyspraxic people also have a range of positive strengths and skills, as outlined at the end of this section. They usually have a number of problems in the following areas.

> *Knowing there is a name for it and that other people are in the same boat really does help me.*
>
> Shirley

Gross motor co-ordination skills (large movements)

- Poor balance – difficulty riding a bicycle and going up and down hills

- Poor posture and fatigue – weak muscle tone means they have difficulty in standing for a long time, floppy, unstable round the joints, flat feet

- Poor integration of the two sides of the body, leading to difficulty with sports that involve jumping and cycling

- Poor hand-eye co-ordination, which causes difficulty with team sports, especially those that involve catching a ball and batting; and difficulties with driving a car

- Lack of rhythm shown in activities such as dancing and aerobics

- Clumsy gait and movement

- Difficulty in changing direction, stopping and starting movements

- Exaggerated 'accessory movements' such as flapping arms when running

- Tendency to fall, trip, bump into things and people

- Probably late reaching the milestones of childhood, such as sitting, crawling (often not crawling at all) and walking.

Dyspraxia is thought to affect up to 10 per cent of the population

Fine motor co-ordination skills (small movements)

- Lack of manual dexterity – poor at two-handed tasks (e.g. problems with using cutlery; domestic chores such as cleaning, cooking, ironing; playing musical instruments and doing craft work)

- Poor manipulative skills – difficulty with typing, handwriting and drawing

- A poor pen grip, pressing too hard when writing, difficulty when writing along a line

- Inadequate grasp – difficulty using tools and domestic implements, difficulty dealing with locks and keys
- Difficulty with dressing and grooming (putting on makeup, shaving, doing hair, fastening clothes, tying shoelaces)
- Poorly established hand dominance – may use right or left hand for different tasks at different times.

Speech and language

- May have been late learning to talk and may speak in an unclear way
- May talk continuously, repeat themselves and interrupt; some people with dyspraxia have difficulty organising the content and sequence of their speech
- Uncontrolled pitch, volume and rate of speech
- Unable to pronounce some words
- Difficulty listening to and understanding speech, especially in large groups.

Eye movements

- Tracking – difficulty in following a moving object smoothly with eyes without excessive head movement; tendency to lose the place while reading
- Poor relocating – cannot look quickly and effectively from one object to another (e.g. looking from a television to a magazine)
- Tendency to blink or squint.

Perception

- Poor visual perception
- Over-sensitivity to light
- Difficulty distinguishing sounds/screening them from background noise
- Tendency to be over-sensitive to noise

Adults with dyspraxia will tend to have more than their fair share of co-ordination and perceptual difficulties

- Difficulty picking up non-verbal signals and in judging tone and pitch of voice in themselves or others
- Difficulties listening and understanding, especially in large groups
- Tendency to take things literally and not understand nuances
- Over- or under-sensitive to touch, which can result in dislike of being touched and/or an aversion to over-loose or tight clothing
- Over- or under-sensitive to smell and taste, pain, extremes of temperature
- Lack of awareness of body position in space and spatial relationships with objects, which can result in bumping into objects and tripping over, spilling and dropping things
- Little sense of time, speed, distance or weight
- Inadequate sense of direction
- Poor at map-reading
- Difficulty in distinguishing left from right.

Learning, thought and memory

- Difficulty in planning and organising thought
- Poor memory – especially short-term memory. May forget and lose things
- Unfocused and erratic. Can be messy and cluttered
- Poor sequencing, causing problems with maths, spelling and essay writing
- Accuracy problems – difficulty with copying movements, sounds, writing, and proofreading
- Difficulty with following instructions, especially more than one at a time
- Difficulty with concentration, may be easily distracted

- May do only one thing at a time properly, though may try to do many things at once
- Slow to finish a task
- May day-dream and wander about aimlessly.

Secondary signs – Emotional and behavioural reactions

Having dyspraxia frequently causes people to become anxious and lacking in self-confidence. This can lead to a range of emotional and behavioural reactions, including:

- tactlessness and frequent interrupting
- problems with team work
- slowness to adapt to new or unpredictable situations, sometimes avoiding them altogether
- impulsiveness – tendency to be easily frustrated, wanting immediate gratification
- tendency to opt out of things that are too difficult
- tendency to get stressed, depressed and anxious easily
- difficulty sleeping
- proneness to emotional outbursts, phobias, fears, obsessions, compulsions, irritability and addictive behaviour.

Positive aspects

However, the picture is by no means all negative. Having to live with dyspraxia usually produces a variety of positive strengths and skills. As a result, many people with dyspraxia are creative, determined, original and hard-working. They also develop strategic-thinking and problem-solving skills. They can also be very caring and intuitive. Others have become gifted writers, such as Victoria Biggs (see her book *Caged in Chaos*, details on p.22).

Associated conditions

In the experience of DANDA, people with dyspraxia can also be prone to depression and/or high levels of anxiety; eczema; asthma; epilepsy; food intolerances, particularly of dairy products and gluten; and digestive problems.

So...do you have dyspraxia?

You may have read through these lists with the dawning recognition 'That's me!' If you can put a tick against 90 per cent of the symptoms or more, particularly those that affect gross and fine co-ordination skills, this is an indication that you may have dyspraxia.

People with dyspraxia tend to be 'one-offs' – creative and original thinkers who work hard for their successes

Further on in this book there are descriptions of difficulties that people with dyspraxia face in specific situations and some of their personal stories. Reading these accounts may confirm once and for all that you have the condition.

Some of the symptoms may indicate that you could be suffering from other conditions such as depression or myalgic encephalomyelitis (ME). If you are at all worried about individual symptoms, it is advisable to visit your GP.

You might want to show this book to a relative or friend – or you might want to put it away and think for a while. Realising that you may have dyspraxia could make you see very differently the influences which have shaped your personality, the way that you live your life, and the relationships you have with family and friends. It may take time to come to terms with your realisation and to decide what, if any, action you want to take.

Do please remember that you are not alone. About one person in ten is thought to have dyspraxia or DCD to some extent – people of all ages and abilities. What is more, people with dyspraxia tend to be 'one-offs' – creative and original thinkers who work hard for their successes.

Dyspraxia is increasingly recognised as a condition in children, but there is still little public recognition of the problem of dyspraxia in adults. DANDA is working to develop under-standing of the specific ways that the condition affects adults. There is a long way to go.

There are no cures for dyspraxia, but you can take practical steps to minimise the impact of the symptoms and learn strate-gies in order to cope with the day-to-day difficulties you experi-ence. This book is intended as a guide to ways of coping with the many problems, big and small, that dyspraxia creates in our everyday lives.

There are no cures for dyspraxia, but you can take practical steps to minimise the impact of the symptoms

> *Being an adult with dyspraxia is like starting out on a big, noisy motorway. At the beginning everyone seems to be going in the same direction. But we dyspraxics don't understand the signposts and suddenly lots of obstacles appear. We have to stop and take a detour, and hope that we will catch up with the others later. Some of us never get back onto the motorway. Instead we get onto the B roads and end up in a village with no way out.*
>
> Ceri

The Adolescent with Developmental Co-ordination Disorder (DCD) by Amanda Kirby (2003). London: Jessica Kingsley Publishers.

The Adult Dyslexic: Interventions and Outcomes by David McLoughlin, Carol Leather and Patricia Stringer (2002). London: Whurr.

Adults with Developmental Co-ordination Disorder by Sharon Drew (2005). London: Whurr.

Caged in Chaos – A Dyspraxic Guide to Breaking Free by Victoria Biggs (2005). London: Jessica Kingsley Publishers.

Coping with Dyspraxia by Jill Eckersley (2004). London: Sheldon Press.

Developmental Dyspraxia Identification and Intervention: A Manual for Parents and Professionals by Madeleine Portwood (1999, second edition). London: David Fulton Publishers. Includes a chapter about adults.

Dyslexia and Stress edited by T.R. Miles and V. Varma (2004, second edition). London: Whurr.

Dyspraxia: The Hidden Handicap by Amanda Kirby (1999). London: Souvenir Press. Includes two chapters aimed at adolescents and adults who have dyspraxia.

Dyspraxic Voices – Adult Experiences of Dyspraxia and Related Conditions edited by Nicola Werenowska (2003). London: DANDA.

Guide to Dyspraxia and Developmental Coordination Disorders by Amanda Kirby and Sharon Drew (2003). London: David Fulton Publishers.

Making Dyslexia Work for You by Vicki Goodwin and Bonita Thomson (2004). London: David Fulton Publishers. Includes CD-ROM.

Perceptuo-Motor Difficulties: Theory and Strategies to Help Children, Adolescents and Adults by Dorothy Penso (1993). London: Chapman and Hall.

Provision for Specific Learning Difficulties – (Key Solutions Series) by Jan Poustie (2001). Taunton: Next Generation.

That's The Way I Think: Dyslexia and Dyspraxia Explained by David Grant (2005). London: David Fulton Publishers.

Understanding Developmental Dyspraxia: A Textbook for Students and Professionals by Madeleine Portwood (2000). London: David Fulton Publishers.

You Mean I'm Not Lazy, Stupid or Crazy. A Self-help Book for Adults with Attention Deficit Disorder by Kate Kelly and Peggy Ramundo (2006). London: Simon and Schuster. Many of the strategies mentioned here will be useful for adults with dyspraxia.

ADDISS. Tel: 020 8906 9068, www.addiss.co.uk. Supports people with attention deficit disorder.

Adult Dyslexia Organisation (ADO). Tel: 020 7297 3911, www.adultdyslexia.org.

AFASIC. Tel: 020 7490 9410 (admin), 0845 355 5577 (helpline), www.afasic.org.uk. Specialist organisation for overcoming speech impairments.

British Dyslexia Association. Tel: 0118 966 8271 (helpline), www.bdadyslexia.org.uk. Can provide details of your local group for adults with dyslexia. You may meet people there who have co-ordination, organisational and concentration disorders.

British Epilepsy Association. Tel: 0808 800 5050 (helpline), www.epilepsy.org.uk.

DANDA. Tel: 020 7435 7891, www.danda.org.uk.

Depression Alliance. Tel: 0845 123 2320, www.depressionalliance.org.

Dyscovery Centre. Tel: 01633 432 330 www.dyscoverycentre.co.uk. For assessments.

Dyspraxia Foundation. Tel: 01462 455016 (admin), 454986 (helpline), www.dyspraxiafoundation.org.uk.

National Asthma Campaign. Tel: 0845 701 0203, www.asthma.org.uk.

National Autistic Society. Tel: 020 7833 2299, 0845 070 4004 (helpline), www.nas.org.uk.

National Eczema Society. Tel: 020 7281 3553 (admin), 0870 241 3604 (helpline, 8am–8pm Mon–Fri), www.eczema.org.uk.

No Panic. Tel: 0808 808 0545 (helpline), www.nopanic.co.uk. For support for anxiety attacks and obsessive-compulsive disorder.

I often commit some terrible 'faux pas' before my brain has realised what I've done.

Karen

Chapter 2

ASSESSMENT, DIAGNOSIS AND TREATMENT

If you have read the symptoms of dyspraxia in Chapter 1 and thought, 'That's me!', you may be asking yourself, 'How can I find out if I really have dyspraxia? If so, what can I do about it?'

There are several paths to assessment and diagnosis and a range of treatments and therapies which can alleviate the various manifestations of dyspraxia.

If you think you could have dyspraxia, you may want this self-assessment confirmed through assessment and diagnosis by an expert in the field. It can be a great relief to be diagnosed as having a known medical condition. Diagnosis can put people in touch with facets of themselves and help them to understand their actions in the past.

For many people, diagnosis is an important step towards obtaining practical help with everyday living. If the condition is severe enough, they can also receive assistance in getting the disability benefits to which they may be entitled (see Appendix 1).

Other people may want to confirm their self-diagnosis for their own peace of mind and to start to investigate ways to overcome specific difficulties that their dyspraxia causes.

First steps

Depending on your personal situation, there are various possible routes to consider.

GP

General practitioners **may** be able to refer you to a clinical psychologist (though many know very little about the condition) for assessment. They may also be able to arrange assessments by other specialists, such as occupational therapists.

For many people diagnosis is an important step towards obtaining practical help

Visiting your doctor to talk about your difficulties and to ask for a referral on the NHS can seem daunting. Your GP may not know a great deal about developmental dyspraxia. However, he or she **could** be the gateway to assessment, diagnosis and possible treatment. Before you attend your appointment, write down anything you may want to say. Providing such a record for the GP is helpful as appointment time is usually limited. If you are not happy with the outcome of your surgery visit, you could register with another GP or obtain a second opinion. Your persistence may pay off.

However, be prepared for the fact that because their knowledge of the condition may be limited, the GP or clinical psychologist may not be as understanding or helpful as you would wish. (Some have failed to diagnose a condition which was later shown to exist.)

Social services

Your local health authority and social services have statutory legal duties and responsibilities to assess an individual's needs, under the NHS and Community Care Act 1990. You can therefore ask for your needs to be assessed by your local social services department. However, they, too, may not be as knowledgeable or helpful as you would wish.

Employment service (Jobcentre Plus network)

If you are unemployed or are experiencing problems with employment, there may be a disability employment adviser at your local Jobcentre Plus who can help. He/she might refer you to an occupational psychologist who may assess you by using a series of tests. These may include psychometric and practical exercises which are designed to find out what skills you have and which jobs you are likely to be good at.

College/university

If you are in further or higher education, there is usually a process by which you can be referred to a specialist. The Learning Support Centre, Special Needs Department or Student Disability Service at your college or university may be able to refer students to a psychologist who has a special interest in dyslexia and specific learning difficulties. The Learning Support Centre will be able to assess you for dyspraxia in relation to your educational needs only.

Many adults with dyspraxia are assessed and diagnosed privately

Private assessment

You may also consider paying for a private assessment. DANDA may be able to suggest appropriate specialists for you to see on a private basis. There are many kinds of specialist who assess for dyspraxia (see p.28).

Each specialist tests for a different aspect of dyspraxia. No single specialist looks at the whole person. Assessment and diagnosis by professionals in more than one discipline would enable you to build up a rounded picture of how dyspraxia affects you. Costs of private consultation vary according to where you live, and the individual specialist. You can expect to pay at least £200 for private assessment and diagnosis by one specialist.

What to do when you first seek assessment

Unless you are going for a private assessment, you may need to prepare to fight your case. You should remember the following:

- Before you keep your appointment, make a firm commitment to yourself: you will achieve your goal.

- Collect together information about dyspraxia to take with you. A list of symptoms, such as the one in the previous chapter, is particularly helpful.

- Try to find the name of someone who knows about dyspraxia at your local hospital, college or Jobcentre. DANDA may be able to help you find appropriate contacts.

- Take along a friend or relative to support you. Tell them about your goal.

- Be firm but polite. You might begin by saying something like, 'I experience a lot of difficulties with everyday tasks/studying/work. I would like to see a specialist who can test for and diagnose dyspraxia. I believe these difficulties may be caused by dyspraxia.'

Each specialist tests for a different aspect of dyspraxia

- Your approach at this stage is very important. Emphasise that you are facing many difficulties and that you really need help.

Who can assess for dyspraxia?

The following specialists can make assessments for, and diagnose dyspraxia:

- psychologists – educational, occupational, neuro-, or clinical

- neurologists – mainly concerned with acquired dyspraxia

- paediatricians who specialise in developmental disorders.

These specialists assess specific areas of difficulty:

- occupational therapists

- physiotherapists

- speech therapists

- behavioural optometrists

- teachers/tutors (see p.97).

Assessment by a psychologist

The assessment which most adults undergo when visiting a psychologist is the Wechsler Adult Intelligence Scales (WAIS). This can reveal a pattern of weaknesses and strengths typical of dyspraxia.

The WAIS is a series of tests which measure your cognitive ability and create a psychometric profile. Some of the tests may be timed; your assessor should explain the format of the tests clearly during the session.

The WAIS tests are divided into two sections – verbal, and performance. The verbal section includes tests to define words and general knowledge questions, and repeating a series of digits forwards or backwards. As part of the performance section you will be asked to reproduce a series of two-dimensional patterns in three dimensions using red and white blocks. Many people with dyspraxia find this test particularly hard. Another particularly difficult test is the copying of symbols under numbers, which involves good co-ordination and concentration skills.

> *Developmental Dyspraxia Identification and Intervention: A Manual for Parents and Professionals* by Madeleine Portwood (1999, second edition). London: David Fulton Publishers. For information on the WAIS and research she has carried out with adults. Also details of the screening and intervention programme devised by the author, which some adults have found helpful.

Psychologists may also take a case history, look at your handwriting and carry out motor skills tests.

Assessment by a neurologist or paediatrician

People who have been assessed by neurologists have been asked to copy a series of gestures and movements, such as putting each finger against the thumb of the same hand, and walking heel to toe. They have also had their case history recorded. Some have been given a full examination to ascertain whether there is likely to be another cause of their difficulties. A few patients have had brain scans. This is because neurologists are normally trained to detect acquired dyspraxia (e.g. as a result of a stroke) rather than developmental dyspraxia, which has been there since birth.

Some paediatricians who specialise in child development will see adult patients privately. Occasionally GPs refer adults to paediatricians on the NHS.

Assessment by an occupational therapist

Occupational therapists look at how the individual copes with activities of daily living and assess them mainly through observation.

Some adults have undergone standardised tests such as the Assessment of Processing Motor Skills (AMPS), which includes cooking and serving a meal according to a strict sequence of instructions. Another test sometimes in use is the BADS (Behavioural Assessment of Disexecutive Syndrome), which entails, for example, finding your way around a map of a zoo by following a sequence of precise instructions. The Morrison F. Gardner Test of Visual-Motor Skills may also be used. It involves copying increasingly complex geometric shapes.

Your GP might refer you to an occupational therapist, medical doctor or clinical psychologist

The emphasis of occupational therapy is on using assessment to improve function, thus making the patient more able, rather than on diagnosis.

There are a number of other tests (see full list in Appendix 3). Many of the tests can be used by college and university tutors to help screen for dyspraxia.

Assessment by a physiotherapist

A physiotherapist's assessment may be appropriate if you have poor posture, low muscle tone, problems with whole-body movements, lack of balance, lack of awareness of yourself in a space, bad memory or poor co-ordination and planning skills.

Assessment by a speech therapist

Speech and language therapists assess for the articulation of words, and the speed and pitch at which they are delivered. They also look at communication skills – the way that something is said, as well as non-verbal skills such as facial expressions, posture and gesture. Most of the assessment is done through observation rather than by formal testing.

Assessment by a behavioural optometrist

Behavioural optometry investigates the adequacy of an individual's visual processing skills – the ability to select and focus on an object with both eyes simultaneously, hold it in focus, and select and focus on another object.

Even if you have good eyesight, you may have visual-processing problems. Perhaps you lose your place when reading unless you track with a finger; or move your head a lot when you look around. Or you may often shut one eye or squint, or experience headaches, concentration difficulties and fatigue.

Adults are assessed by a behavioural optometrist to see how well their eyes work together. They are tested on spatial awareness, spatial relationships and depth perception, and to see whether their eye movements are slow, uncoordinated or require a great deal of effort.

IRLEN SYNDROME

Some people have been tested for Irlen or scotopic sensitivity disorder syndrome, which can make print appear to be distorted or blurred, especially on a white background. There is plenty of anecdotal evidence of this syndrome and its links with dyspraxia, but no scientific proof as yet. People with this syndrome are thought to be over-sensitive to light. Many who have the symptoms of this syndrome have been helped by using different coloured overlays on printed text.

After assessment and diagnosis you should receive a written report from your assessor

What happens after assessment and diagnosis?

You should receive a written report from your assessor. If you were referred by your GP, he or she will receive a copy as well. Occasionally, the assessor will only send the report to your GP. You have a right to look at this information, so contact your surgery and ask to see it.

If you are diagnosed as having moderate to severe dyspraxia, your local Citizens Advice Bureau, welfare rights office or advocacy service may be able to advise on benefits for which you are eligible (see Appendix 1).

Students can obtain advice from their college's Learning Support Centre or its equivalent: see Chapter 7 for details of the kinds of assistance available.

> *Being diagnosed with dyspraxia removed some of the feelings of guilt I had suffered. I had a problem and like a general on the battlefield I had identified the enemy and was evaluating its strengths and weaknesses as well as my own.*
>
> Mike

Treatment and intervention

Psycho-therapy and counselling can be used to raise self-esteem

The specialist who diagnoses you may refer you for treatment or may ask your GP to do so. A diagnosis obtained through the NHS does not guarantee that you will receive treatment. If you are allocated NHS treatment, you may have to wait a long time. If this is the case, you might want to consider paying for private treatment.

If you have been assessed privately you can refer yourself for private treatment. However, professionals who treat adults with dyspraxia are very thin on the ground.

Occupational therapists, physiotherapists, speech thera-pists and behavioural optometrists are likely to be able to treat you themselves after assessment.

DANDA does not endorse any individual treatment. It is up to individuals to choose what is best for them in their own circum-stances.

Psychotherapy

Diagnosis of dyspraxia is not always an unmitigated relief. People often feel angry that their diagnosis has come so late, and they can find it hard to come to terms with their new status as a person with dyspraxia.

Psychotherapy and counselling can be used to raise self-esteem. Not everybody who has dyspraxia needs counsel-ling as they may have received sufficient support from their family, school and colleagues, or their particular type of dyspraxia may have had minimal impact on their lives. However, the majority of people who have dyspraxia suffer from damaged self-esteem, having faced hostility and disbelief all their lives. Many have endured accusations of being lazy and stupid and have experienced constant failure.

Cognitive-behavioural therapy has proved particularly useful for people with specific learning difficulties. The crux of this therapy is that altering negative and unrealistic thinking can reduce emotional disturbance. This is a practical rather than a 'talking' therapy, and aims to teach clients the skills they need to identify and modify self-defeating thoughts and beliefs.

> **i** No Panic provides a lay-person self-help cognitive and behavioural therapy as a basis for recovery. Tel: freephone 0808 808 0545 for further information.
>
> The British Association of Behavioural and Cognitive Psychotherapists can put you in touch with a private therapist near you. The therapy is also available on the NHS. Tel: 01254 875277, www.bacp.co.uk for a list of practitioners in your area.

Occupational therapy

Occupational therapists focus on the skills you need to cope with everyday life. They find out which tasks you find difficult and teach strategies to help you to cope with them. They may also help you to acquire organisational skills and teach cooking or crafts, or provide equipment such as kettle tippers and jar openers. An occupational therapist may also suggest exercises to strengthen manual dexterity and finger co-ordination and to improve visual perception. An occupational therapist from your local social services department may assess adaptations to your home. You may be entitled to a means-tested Disability Facilities Grant to enable the adaptations to be carried out. Some of these adaptations are described in Chapter 6.

Occupational therapists focus on the skills you need to cope with everyday life

I had eight months of occupational therapy. My first sessions concentrated on cookery, to help to improve my organisational skills and breaking down of tasks, and to provide a sense of achievement. I also did art and craft activities which helped to build up my concentration, accuracy and fine motor skills. I had an assessment every six to eight weeks to monitor the progress of treatment. Now I can do several practical things at the same time, which I never used to be able to cope with.

Judith

Physio-therapy can help with hand-eye co-ordination and with spatial awareness

Some people with dyspraxia have undergone **sensory integra-tion**, which is a specialised form of occupational therapy. It is based on the premise that people with dyspraxia may have a dysfunctional sensory system, so that messages received from your senses are not integrated or organised appropriately in the brain. Varying degrees of problems in development information processing and behaviour may result. Treatment consists mainly of physical exercises.

Physiotherapy

Members of DANDA have been to physiotherapists who have devised programmes of exercises which strengthen the shoulders, to help with fine motor skills such as handwriting. They have also exercised to strengthen their pelvic girdle, which improves balance and ball kicking.

Physiotherapy can also help with hand-eye co-ordination and with spatial awareness.

Speech therapy

Speech therapy undertaken by members of the Group has covered help with the principles of non-verbal communication (see Chapter 4 for more about this), training in social skills, training in breathing and relaxing effectively, and exercises to help with awareness of the volume, pitch and tone of speech as well as improvements to articulation.

Behavioural optometry

Some members have undergone visual therapy, a structured programme which is designed to develop efficient and comprehensive visual processing. Exercises may include the use of a special concave lens held to each eye in turn to help to control focus.

Help!

DANDA can give you information about private therapists and some who work within the NHS. Write to or telephone the Group – details are on p.163.

Other treatments and interventions

Medication and food supplements

GPs and psychiatrists may prescribe medication for depression and anxiety. These closely related conditions may be triggered by the symptoms of dyspraxia and can increase those symptoms in a vicious spiral. Depression and anxiety make concentration difficult, and disrupt sleep. You may completely lose your appetite, or binge-eat. You may also feel very misunderstood.

Anti-depressants can help, and are not addictive. Alternatively you may prefer to take herbal remedies or supplements such as St John's wort, ginseng, etc.

There has recently been much research to show that highly unsaturated fatty acids (HUFA), such as those found in oily fish (e.g. salmon, sardines and tuna), can help some people with dyspraxia and other specific learning difficulties. This is because many people with these conditions have a deficiency of fatty acids, which have been proved to help with eye and brain function. Signs of fatty-acid deficiency include excessive thirst, frequent urination, dry hair, skin and nails, as well as allergies such as eczema and asthma. The essential fatty acids are omega-6 and omega-3 and can be found in supplements such as Eye-Q and MorEPA (which contains virgin fish oils and evening primrose oil). Eye Q can be obtained or ordered from

DANDA can give you information

most chemists. MorEPA can be obtained from Heathly and Essential www.healthlyandessential.com, tel: 08700 536000.

You should always tell your GP if you take herbal remedies or supplements as they may interact with other medication.

Conductive education

This system, originally devised chiefly to help people with cerebral palsy, teaches groups and individuals to break down into easy steps the everyday tasks they find difficult. Through succeeding with these tasks, confidence and self-esteem are increased. Conductive education may be available to you through the NHS.

Neuro-physiological psychology

Therapies and exercise systems can alleviate the symptoms of dyspraxia

The Institute for Neuro-Physiological Psychology sees dyspraxia as one of the symptoms of neuro-developmental delay. This means that the primitive reflexes with which everyone is born and which usually disappear within the first year of life are not inhibited in a dyspraxic person as they should be. These reflexes remain 'active' and may impede motor control, eye functions, hand-eye co-ordination, and perceptual skills.

The Institute carries out neurological tests and devises a programme of movements to correct the reflexes, to be carried out each day. Treatment by the Institute is not currently available through the NHS.

Complementary therapies

Therapies such as aromatherapy and exercise systems such as tai chi can help you to relax and alleviate the symptoms of dyspraxia. See the next chapter for ideas on different ways to relax.

Developmental Dyspraxia Identification and Intervention: A Manual for Parents and Professionals by Madeleine Portwood (1999, second edition). London: David Fulton Publishers.

These organisations will provide lists of private practitioners:

British Association of Behavioural Optometrists. Tel: 01242 602689, www.babo.co.uk.

British Association of Counselling and Psychotherapy. Tel: 0870 443 5252, www.bacp.co.uk.

British Association/College of Occupational Therapists. Tel: 020 7357 6480, www.cot.co.uk.

British Psychological Society. Tel: 0116 254 9568, www.bps.org.uk.

Chartered Society of Physiotherapy. Tel: 020 7306 6666, www.csp.org.uk.

Royal College of Speech and Language Therapists. Tel: 020 7378 1200, www.rcslt.org.uk.

Other organisations:

The Dyscovery Centre. Tel: 01633 432 330, www.dyscovery.co.uk.

Foundation for Conductive Education. Tel: 0121 449 1569, www.conductive-education.org.uk.

Institute for Neuro-Physiological Psychology. Tel: 01244 311414, www.inpp.org.uk.

Chapter 3

RELAXATION, SPORTS AND EXERCISE

People who have dyspraxia often suffer greater levels of stress than the average person, so relaxing leisure pursuits are particularly important for us.

We are all different. Some people find that passive pursuits, such as aromatherapy, are the most relaxing, whereas others prefer physical activities to help them to unwind. The symptoms of dyspraxia can make some activities unsuitable. For example, people with dyspraxia may have difficulty participating in team games. Others dislike being touched by another person and so find massage unpleasant.

When choosing sports and leisure activities, you might want to bear in mind:

- Team games usually require instant responses to the actions of other team members and quick reactions.

- Team games usually require participants to be doing more than one thing at the same time – watching the ball, monitoring the movements of other players and organising your own movements.

- Activities which involve competition can affect your self-esteem. You may find that co-operative pursuits are more beneficial.

- Many solitary sports allow participants ample time for planning movements, mentally and physically.

- Solitary sports such as golf, archery and darts do not require swift reactions to the movements of others. You can compete against yourself.

- Exercise systems which entail complex sequences of movement, such as aerobics, or which require speedy responses, are unlikely to be helpful for people with dyspraxic characteristics.

- Exercise systems that require a group of people to undertake synchronised movements, such as rowing or dance routines, are likely to prove difficult.

Relax!

Relaxation techniques help our minds to focus on our bodies in a positive way. These can be combined with therapies that specifically treat the symptoms of dyspraxia and with sports and exercise.

There are many relaxation tapes on the market. Ask around for recommendations, borrow and try them.

People with dyspraxia may have difficulty participating in team games

This exercise makes use of visualisation and positive thinking and is recommended for people with dyspraxia by Dianne Zaccheo, a medical social worker who specialises in developmental disorders.

First, start to relax:

- Take the phone off the hook and shut out as many distractions as you can.

- Select a piece of music that you find particularly calming.

- Settle down in a comfy chair in a relaxed but upright position. Shut your eyes and concentrate on the soles of your feet.

- Start to breathe deeply. Imagine you are drawing breath from the soles of your feet.

Continued on next page

Continued from previous page

- Store your breath in your diaphragm for about 15 seconds. Exhale slowly. As you breathe out, feel yourself relax.

Then you can start to visualise the scene:

- You are walking through your favourite place. First you see just your feet moving. Then your arms are swinging and your whole body moving along. A small speck is moving towards you from a distance, and as it slowly spreads out it takes the form of a mountain.

- You are face to face with the mountain. You step on to the path through the foothills at the bottom of the mountain. Slowly you gain height, and as you go higher you look back behind you and notice the irritations, the obstacles and the difficulties in your life slowly falling away. You've left them behind and you see them far away beneath you in the foothills. You keep climbing higher and higher, up to the top of the mountain.

- You come out on to a plateau at the top of the mountain. Spreading out beneath you into the far distance is a beautiful vista of sunlit landscape. You've arrived at the place you want to be. Take a minute or two to see yourself doing the things you want to do in your life. Then slowly breathe out, let your eyes open and return calm and refreshed to reality.

Relaxation techniques help our minds to focus on our bodies in a positive way

Relaxation (101 Essential Tips) by Nitya Lacroix and Deni Brown (1998). London: Dorling Kindersley. A neat little book with suggestions of many types of therapies.

Complementary therapies

All of these therapies have been found to help people with dyspraxia. They are just some of the possibilities available. You may find others which are just as beneficial.

These therapies can be tried by anyone. They are meant to be fun and relaxing. If you find any of them difficult or distressing in any way, just stop doing them! If you have any doubts about their suitability, consult an expert in the field or your GP.

For information on local practitioners of all types of complementary therapy contact the Complementary Medical Association, 67 Eagle Heights, The Falcons, Bramlands Close, London SW11 2LJ. Tel: 0845 1298434, www.the-cma.org.uk.

Alexander Technique

The Alexander Technique trains your internal feedback system to recognise tension and to become more aware of your balance, posture and movement. It can be extremely relaxing and teaches how to co-ordinate mind and body effectively. The technique is taught through a course of individual lessons or at evening classes.

After ten minutes' treatment I was a different person. I was fully relaxed in a way I had not experienced before. I was also able to talk in a quiet voice — something I find very difficult to do normally. I am sure that more lessons would help me to be more relaxed and to improve my co-ordination.

Mary

These therapies can be tried by anyone. They are meant to be fun and relaxing

i   Society of Teachers of the Alexander Technique (STAT), Ist Floor, Linton House, 39–51 Highgate Road, London NW5 1RS. Tel: 0845 2307828, www.stat.org.uk.

Aromatherapy

Treatment with essential oils through inhalation or massage can relieve anxiety and help with depressive disorders. You should start to feel the benefit after one or two sessions.

Responses to the oils are highly individual. Some people with dyspraxia are extremely sensitive to smell and the oils may cause allergies, so it is a good idea to consult a trained aromatherapist about the best oils for you.

Massage

Massage is a particularly good way of getting aromatherapy oils into the bloodstream. On its own, it helps relax the muscles and increase blood circulation around the body and therefore improves your energy levels. Any stiffness or tightness in the muscles can be alleviated by massage.

Music

The right music – particularly certain types of classical music – can improve learning, memory, behaviour and organization as well as clarity of thought. It can also relieve the stress of being ill.

 www.mozarteffect.com

Treatment with essential oils through inhalation or massage can relieve anxiety

Reflexology

Reflexology's theory is that the organs of the body are reflected in the nerve centres of the feet: by stimulating these through massage, particularly of the soles and sides of the feet, it is possible to bring about a reaction in corresponding parts of the body.

Reflexology is a simple treatment that can be used to locate and treat areas of dysfunction or imbalance in the body.

 Association of Reflexologists, 5 Fore Street, Taunton, Somerset TA1 1HX. Tel: 0870 567 3320, www.aor.org.uk.

Tai chi

Tai chi or tai chi chuan is an ancient Chinese system of physical exercise based on the principles of effortless breathing, rhythmic movement and balance of weight. Although it is known as a form of self-defence, it is practised today as a means of co-ordinating mind, body and spirit by building inner confidence. It is possible to achieve greater clarity of thought and heightened awareness of oneself, which can be called upon in times of stress or uncertainty. Classes are available in most areas.

 Simply Tai Chi Book and DVD by Graham Bryant and Lorraine James (2004). Dingley, VIC: Hinckler Books.

www.taichifinder.co.uk. Tel: 0845 890 0744

Yoga

Yoga is an ancient discipline which offers the possibility of physical, mental and emotional health. It is also a type of meditation which is achieved by the practice of postures with breathing, concentration and relaxation techniques.

The results of practising yoga can be increased co-ordination, flexibility, improved posture and breathing, as well as the ability to focus and relax. It can help with shedding aches and pains in the muscles and joints. It is suitable for everyone, at every stage of life.

You learn yoga at classes. Do not try the exercises on your own as you might strain yourself. There are many different types of yoga; it is best to try them to see which one you benefit from most.

Yoga is suitable for everyone, at every stage of life

 British Wheel of Yoga, 25 Jermyn Street, Sleaford, Lincs NG34 7RU. Tel: 01529 306851, www.bwy.org.uk. For details of Hatha Yoga around the country.

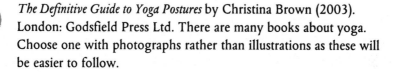 *The Definitive Guide to Yoga Postures* by Christina Brown (2003). London: Godsfield Press Ltd. There are many books about yoga. Choose one with photographs rather than illustrations as these will be easier to follow.

Sports and exercise

Experiences at school have turned many people with dyspraxia away from participating in sports. However, undertaking a form of physical activity which is interesting and rewarding will help to improve body image, spatial understanding and posture. Physical exercise will also relieve stress, particularly if you do it out of doors.

> *PE was a nightmare at school as I had difficulty catching balls, hopping, doing gymnastics, climbing and so on. I was always picked last when teams were chosen.*
>
> Clare

Archery improves trunk strength, co-ordination, and distance judgement.

Bowls outdoor and ten pin bowling can be comparatively easy for dyspraxics as they can take their time when participating. Ten pin bowling with the sides left up can be particularly suitable for adults with motor problems.

Experiences at school have turned many people with dyspraxia away from sports

Croquet helps with spatial awareness and distance judgement. It is cerebral as well as reasonably physical.

Darts improves distance judgement and is easy to do at home.

Golf improves distance judgement and is a sport where you beat your own record, out in the open.

Horse-riding is excellent for developing balance, improving posture and strengthening muscle tone. It also helps with following instructions and distinguishing right from left. Grooming and saddling a horse involves developing organisational skills in a pleasant environment. Your local Riding for the Disabled Association may be able to help you to take up horse-riding. They are likely to be patient and understanding and tend to use particularly placid horses.

 Riding for the Disabled Association, Lavinia Norfolk House, Avenue R, National Agriculture Centre, Stoneleigh Park, Warwickshire CV8 2LY. Tel: 0845 658 1082, www.riding-for-disabled.org.uk.

Martial arts such as aikido, judo, karate and taekwondo can help with co-ordination and ease stress.

Pilates is a system of gentle exercises which can help to integrate mind, body and spirit. Pilates should help you with your breathing, co-ordination, concentration, posture and muscle tone and exercise and/or relax you.

Snooker helps with spatial awareness and hand-eye co-ordination.

Water sports, such as canoeing, rowing (on your own, rather than in a team) and swimming, can help to give equal power and range of movement to both sides of the body.

Exercising for fitness

I am a member of a health club where I use the gym and swimming pool. I find this very benefical.

Martin

Ordinary aerobics can be too fast and complex

Aquarobics are a series of exercises in water, performed to music. It is suitable for everybody. Ordinary aerobics can be too fast and complex for some dyspraxics.

Gym exercise at your own pace is ideal – there is time to plan your movements and consider your position in space and in relation to the equipment. It also builds up your muscle tone. Weight-lifting can also be good for this.

Both gym exercise and weight-lifting should only be carried out under strict supervision in order to avoid injury.

Walking and running are ideal for beating your own record and improving going up and down hills. It also strengthens your muscles and improves your circulation and breathing – not to mention the benefits of fresh air.

Brain Gym or Educational Kinesiology

Brain Gym is a sensory-motor programme which consists of simple movements to help the co-ordination of eyes, ears, hands and the whole body. Brain Gym's simple movements can integrate the different parts of the brain, leading to whole brain/body learning. For example, crossing the body's midline (as in the exercise cross-crawling) can allow both sides of the brain to work together better. This in turn can reduce stress and improve co-ordination and learning.

 Educational Kinesiology UK Foundation, 12 Golders Rise, Hendon, London NW4 2HR. Tel: 020 8202 9747, www.braingym.org.uk.

> *I've got a degree and a qualification in nursing people with learning disabilities. I also enjoy creative writing and have for the first time learned to enjoy exercise like swimming, yoga and circuit training.*
>
> Clare

Taking part in evening classes and clubs can be soothing and diverting

Relaxing hobbies

Taking part in evening classes and clubs can be soothing and diverting. They may help you to overcome social difficulties as well, as they are excellent opportunities for meeting people.

Art, literature and music appreciation can provide a good escape route from the world of work, routine and worry. People with dyspraxia are often highly visual – so make the most of your aptitude and really enjoy paintings and buildings, or just seek out videos which relate to your hobbies. You could make time too for listening to serene music and for music appreciation. Hobbies may help to ease symptoms of dyspraxia. Learning to play a musical instrument can help to improve fine motor co-ordination. Be careful to choose the right instrument for you – some are more difficult to master than others.

Playing chess or draughts will increase your memory and planning ability.

Many people with dyspraxia find **clay modelling** particularly relaxing and technically not as demanding as some other crafts. Creative work such as **writing, painting** and **photography** can be mentally very relaxing. Adults with dyspraxia often excel at creative writing and photography.

Caring for and working with animals is something that many people with dyspraxia enjoy. Looking after a pet has been proved to increase your life span!

Making things helped me to overcome the problem of distinguishing left from right. It also helped to improve my muscle tone and powers of stamina. Being able to make a stool and a tray improved my self-esteem considerably. Occasionally I still look at them and find it hard to believe that I made them.

Don

Chapter 4

COMMUNICATION AND RELATIONSHIPS

This chapter includes practical hints, thoughts and a wide range of ideas about communication and sustaining relationships.

As you read on, you may well think that some of the thoughts and ideas are mundane and obvious, and even that some seem silly. They are included because people with dyspraxia ask DANDA about them, tackling them as very real difficulties.

The coping strategies and practical tips have all been 'discovered' and used successfully by dyspraxics. A point which appears to you to be obvious, even silly and not worth writing down, could be a revelation to another reader.

People who have dyspraxia and associated conditions are often seen as disruptive, aggressive and uncooperative. The symptoms of dyspraxia include problems with perception, so sufferers are often unaware of the impact of their own behaviour and of the implications of what others are saying and doing. Add in difficulties with co-ordination and voice control, and the whole area of communication and building and sustaining relationships with others becomes fraught.

I often commit some terrible 'faux pas' before my brain has realised what I've done. Sometimes I think that taking everything literally, and alienating other people are my only talents.

Karen

Conversations and discussions

Conversation with a person who has dyspraxia tends to jump from subject to subject. We often go off at a tangent and do not adapt the way that we communicate to accommodate the listener. We tend not to listen to the speaker and constantly interrupt. Sometimes we wait for the other speaker to draw breath and then blurt out ideas we have not thought through.

The way that we communicate can be negative, competitive and self-centred. Our tendency to interrupt and the lack of reciprocity can be frustrating for family, friends and colleagues.

Talking in groups, and interjecting at the right moment can be hard, especially if we are anxious about remembering what we want to express. We may say nothing at all, or we may dominate the conversation completely. Our words tend to pour out in a torrent, and listeners find us hard to understand.

It can be hard for us to integrate new information with previously learned information. We often take on board statements by others before questioning the validity of those statements. If what is said is ambiguous, we often do not ask for clarification.

The way that we communicate can be negative, competitive and self-centred

Sometimes it is like being someone who has just had a stroke. You know what you want to say but somehow it seems to be difficult to find the words when you want them.

Ceri

Understanding humour and sarcasm

People with dyspraxia tend to take things literally and fail to pick up the finer nuances in a conversation. For example, in response to the social pleasantry 'How are you?', you might go into great detail about your recent illnesses. You might also interpret meta-phors, jokes and sarcastic comments in a literal way.

You may feel that the way you talk with other people or your approach to humour and sarcasm are too deeply rooted to change. However, developing your communication skills and getting to grips with the unwritten social rules can be learned to some extent.

How to develop listening skills

- Keep your eyes focused upon the person who is communicating with you. Lack of eye contact can be interpreted by other people as indicative of low self-esteem, dishonesty, or lack of intelligence.

- Don't put your hands in front of your face.

- Consciously stop yourself from fidgeting, yawning, or looking around!

- Try and be sensitive to non-verbal cues (see below).

- Smile and nod to encourage the speaker. Alternatively, make sounds such as 'mm' and 'aha', which will show that you are concentrating on what is being said.

- Encourage the speaker by mirroring their changes in their face and body language. You can mirror what they are saying when you reply.

- When people drop their voice, it usually means that they have finished what they were saying. If they raise their voice at the end of a sentence they are asking a question.

- Courses and classes about counselling can teach you listening skills.

Only 7 per cent of emotional meaning is expressed through words

> *I used to be oblivious to eye contact. Perhaps I was unconsciously avoiding it. I shrank inside myself as I spoke to people. I would avert my eyes and my body language would draw back and become distant.*
>
> *Now sometimes it's as if a challenge goes on between us to hold each other's gaze without flinching. Sometimes I become sloppy. My eyes drift away and I'm vacant, and my body language will tail off.*
>
> Paul

How to develop communication skills

- Be aware of the appropriate time to speak. Choosing the right time and place to bring up a topic can make all the difference between being listened to and being ignored.

- Impulsiveness control and anger control are important skills to master.

- Personal questions and comments make people feel uncomfortable. You need to be aware of the topics of conversation, questions and comments that can cause embarrassment or unease in others.

- You may want to avoid noisy pubs, discos and cafes, especially with groups, as communication can be very difficult in these places.

- Learn to recognise the signs that show you are overstaying your welcome.

Up close and at a distance, your body conveys to others your feelings and attitude

Non-verbal communication

It has been estimated that only 7 per cent of emotional meaning is expressed through words. Serious misunderstandings occur if we fail to interpret non-verbal messages correctly or if we send messages that do not actually reflect our emotions.

POSTURE

Posture is tellingly defined by the Concise Oxford Dictionary as 'carriage, attitude of body'. The way we stand or sit is one of our main means of non-verbal communication, conveying our attitude powerfully.

Many people with dyspraxia have low muscle tone, so it is difficult to maintain a particular position. You may find it hard to stand still for any length of time, or to balance; and you may tend to slouch.

Up close and at a distance, your body conveys to others your feelings and attitude. Knowing the 'meaning' of certain postures will help you to moderate your body language, use it to reflect your feelings and to interpret accurately the signals that someone else's body sends you. Try them out for yourself in front of a full-length mirror!

When the body does this...	...it means
Head down, kicking foot on floor	Defeat
Standing with legs apart and hands on hips	Aggression, anger
Standing hunched over, looking over your shoulder	Fear
Chin raised, hands on hips, staring ahead	Defiance
Comfortably sitting down, slouched slightly, face relaxed	Rest

We are judged by the way we walk. If you can, learn to walk as well as possible, at an even speed and with your head high. Be aware of what your arms are doing, and try to relax them as you walk.

GESTURES

Arms, hands and fingers send many kinds of messages. If you are not aware of your gestures you may well convey the wrong message. You can practise the following gestures and be aware when others make them.

When the gesture is this...	...it means
Shaking a finger	Chastising, warning
Pointing	Pay attention
Finger across throat	Stop, or there'll be big trouble
Clenched fist	Hostility
Arms crossed over the chest	Closed off, not receptive
Palms open	Openness and receptivity

FACIAL EXPRESSIONS

People's faces, especially their mouths and eyes, give us valuable clues about their feelings and attitudes. (You can always tell whether a smile is true or false by looking at the smiler's eyes: in a true smile, the eyes are narrowed.) Eye contact enables you to be visually aware of these clues – but it is important not to stare.

PERSONAL DISTANCE AND TOUCHING

The physical space around people plays a major role in communication. If you get too close, they feel that their space has been invaded. It is a good idea to apologise if you forget about personal distance.

Because we lack spatial awareness and have poor co-ordination we tend to touch other people too vigorously and so communicate a negative rather than a positive message.

Games to help with communication

- Conversations can be rehearsed. You could write a script of the conversation to practise with a friend and build up your confidence.

- As well as trying out postures or gestures, role-play with a friend. See if you can guess what the gesture or expression he or she is making means.

- Turn the sound down while you watch a drama programme on television. See if you can understand what is going on by following just the gestures and facial expressions.

- You may be able to make or borrow a video tape of someone interacting with friends. Analyse it for posture and gesture, and for tone of voice (see below).

Try to be aware of your tone of voice

Appearance

The clothes we wear, how clean they are, and how clean we are, communicate an enormous amount about how we see ourselves. The next chapter gives ideas about choosing clothes and staying clean to present a positive image.

Over-reacting to a situation by laughing or crying too much can be annoying and embarrassing to others

Speech and voice control

Try to be aware of your tone of voice and how loudly and quickly you speak. There may well be a discrepancy between the meaning of what you say and the way you say it – you might speak as if you are in a panic, but feel quite calm inside.

Tone is the most powerful communicator in non-verbal language. Speaking in a low-pitched tone will give you greater authority. When your voice gets loud, listeners may well extend their arms in front of them as if to say, don't come near me.

Slowing down your speech will give you time to modulate your volume and think about what you are saying. If you speak too fast when you are communicating ideas or instructions, people won't understand what you have said. If you speak fast, listeners probably think you are in a rush, or are nervous, or that there is an emergency.

Learning to relax can help you to slow down and quieten your speech. Deep, slow breathing, and practising the Alexander Technique or yoga can all benefit your voice.

Non-verbal sounds as well as words can express different feelings: 'I don't like the taste of this food' can be expressed as 'Yuck'; and 'Oh, I am sorry to hear that' can be expressed as 'Ah'. Some sounds can be irritating or detract from what is being said. Think of a grating laugh, or the sound when you clear your throat. These kinds of sounds should not be used as fillers or as delaying tactics when communicating.

You should also be aware of how the meaning of a sentence can change when different words are emphasised. 'YOU may not go' means everyone else can go except you; whereas 'You may NOT go' means, stay right there.

Over-reacting to a situation by laughing or crying too much can be annoying and embarrassing to others, as can under-reaction. People with perceptuo-motor difficulties often cannot find the 'happy medium' when they react.

Personal and sexual relationships

How we present and conduct ourselves is important in all areas where contact is made with others: within the family, at work, in social situations and in our local community.

The importance of personal appearance for all these relationships has been well documented and there are a number of sources of information on improving personal presentation. There are far fewer resources for finding out how to cope with the symptoms of dyspraxia in our personal, sexual relationships.

The beginning of a relationship may be the most difficult, as subtle approaches are appropriate. You could take advice about eye contact: when it is appropriate to hold a gaze and when you should look away. It may be necessary to spend time planning how, when and where touching is appropriate, and even practise how to touch the other person with gentle, smooth movements.

As your relationship develops it should be possible to discuss difficulties with your partner – although returning continually to the subject of your own co-ordination problems may not help the relationship to flourish! Be sincere but keep the discussion low-key.

With a romantic friendship comes physical intimacy. Sex can involve the whole person, mind and body. You may have difficulty with your own position in space, which may be particularly apparent when your body is in unfamiliar positions. You might have difficulty regulating your movements. You may also have problems with a poor sense of rhythm, or with anticipating the reactions and movements of your partner.

When and how to talk about these problems with your partner can be a big issue. Raising them too early in your relationship could give the impression that you want things to develop quickly – maybe too quickly. On the other hand, leaving problems unvoiced for too long could result in ill feelings on both sides. Choose a time when you both feel happy and contented. Do not overemphasise your difficulties or make a big fuss about them. A loving, tender, understanding relationship will go a long way towards minimising your problems.

It is up to you to communicate your difficulty, on a 'need to know' basis

> *My husband has been a constant source of support. He was aware of my problems from the outset, but instead of holding me back he has always encouraged me to take risks. Without him I'd never have learned to ski or drive.*
>
> Judith

Taking responsibility

Telling people who become close to you about your dyspraxia is one issue – it is part of what has happened to you in the past and who you are now. Quite another issue is the other people you meet from day to day to whom you choose to disclose your condition.

Only you will know about the kinds of difficulties that you endure – and when you start to experience new ones, in new situations. It is up to you to communicate your difficulty, on a 'need to know' basis.

The kinds of situation in which you might experience problems and in which you need immediate help include:

- having X-rays – positioning yourself and staying still may be very hard

- using crutches – problems with maintaining the rhythm of the crutches' movement and with sequencing

- at the physiotherapist – cannot 'move with' him or her during a treatment session

- at the dentist – frequent gagging during treatment. See Chapter 5 for how to deal with this.

You don't have to go into detail about dyspraxia, or even mention it. Just state very clearly the specific problem that you have and, if appropriate, ask if anything can be done to help you.

Do not just say, 'I have dyspraxia' – say what you mean

Giving birth

Childbirth is the event when you need to have confidence in your body, and in your ability to remember and act upon coping techniques. The second stage of labour poses particular problems, as you need to co-ordinate muscle contraction with the force necessary to expel the baby.

You must make your midwife and obstetrician aware that you may have difficulty with the co-ordination skills you will need during childbirth. It will not be sufficient to say, 'I have dyspraxia.' You need to explain how you think that the dyspraxia will affect your co-ordination and planning of movements.

Ante-natal classes can help to prepare you for these movements: you may be able to go to extra classes for additional practice of breathing techniques and co-ordination of the breathing and the muscle contractions.

Telling the staff about your specific difficulties may make a difference to the way you are treated by the midwives and doctors during the birth. It would be a pity to make childbirth – one of the most important events in your life – more difficult than it has to be because the staff were not made aware of your problems.

How I wish I'd known that I was dyspraxic when I gave birth to my children. The second stage of labour was the worst experience of my life. Gas and air made the labour worse because I could not use it properly. All the midwives did was shout at me and tell me how hopeless I was and how the baby was in distress.

Mary

Parenting

The difficulties with organisation, consistency, self-confidence and self-esteem which often accompany perceptuo-motor problems may affect some parents' ability to handle their children. You may need to make a conscious effort to keep continuity in the way you relate to your children, and to help them with organising their play, personal space and life skills.

It will be easier for you to cope with physical tasks as the children get older and more independent, although your problems of consistency and organisation will remain. The children will accept the way you are even when you feel you have come to the end of the line.

You could try:

- helping your children to focus on areas of personal strength to enhance their self-esteem
- remembering always that positive reinforcement builds self-esteem, whereas negative reinforcement destroys it
- trying as hard as you can to be a good role-model
- using the Stop, Think, Act approach for problem solving
- setting goals, and rewarding signs of growth and progress when working towards those goals
- following through, and keeping your promises
- helping your children to name their feelings (use visual aids and role-playing)

You may need to make a conscious effort to keep continuity in the way you relate to your children

- always asking your children to repeat instructions back to you

- preparing your children for what might happen next

- having rewards and consequences for good and bad actions

- presenting a united front approach to parenting with your partner

- drawing up house rules and sticking them on the fridge

- holding a weekly family meeting.

 1–2–3 Magic: Effective Discipline for Children 2–12 by Thomas W. Phelan (2003). Geln Ellen, IL: Child Management Inc.

Self-help groups can give much-needed support and boost self-esteem and confidence

Helping yourself

Self-help groups can give much-needed support and boost self-esteem and confidence. DANDA runs self-help groups in some parts of London: contact them for details.

If there is no group in your area, your local adult education centre may run courses such as assertiveness training, self-development and presentation skills, and positive thinking which may be helpful. Courses on social and communication skills can be useful if you have difficulties in social situations, and with listening to others. A course on counselling techniques can also help you to learn to listen.

Assertiveness training

Learning to be assertive is about standing up for yourself (not being passive) while not infringing the rights of other people (not being aggressive). Assertiveness training is run by many adult education centres and may help you to understand why you behave as you do; to recognise when

your behaviour is counter-productive; and to know what to do about it.

Training can help you to understand other people better, to become more confident, to control your emotions, and to make sure that others do not manipulate you.

Assertiveness by Windy Dryden and Daniel Constantinou (2004). London: Sheldon Press.

Neuro-Linguistic Programming

Neuro-Linguistic Programming is an established programme that can help with creating rapport with others; understanding and using body language; and thinking about and achieving the results you want. The programme is delivered through a number of consultants.

Training should help you to become more confident

NLP Education Network, Jeff Lewis, 24 Oaklands Lane, Smallford, St Albans, Herts AL4 0HR. Tel: 01727 856200, www.new-oceans.co.uk.

Coaching

The attentions of a private coach can help you to develop communication skills. Coaches are also useful to maintain motivation after an initial assessment. Clients are telephoned at pre-arranged intervals and encouraged to complete their agreed targets.

For a trained coach or training in coaching contact the Coaching Academy. Tel: 0800 783 4823, www.the-coaching-academy.co.uk, www.healthutopia.com, or the UK College of Life Coaching, www.cmiexcel.com.

Teaching Your Child the Language of Social Success by Marshall P. Duke, Stephen Nowicki and Elizabeth Martin (1996). Atlanta: Peachtree Publishers. Good for adults as well as children.

How to Talk So People Listen by Sonya Hamlin (1999). London: HarperCollins.

Listening Skills by Ian Mackay (1995). London: Chartered Institute of Personnel and Development.

The Definitive Book of Body Language: How to Read Others' Thoughts by Their Gestures by Allan and Barbara Pease (2005). London: Orion Books.

What Does Everybody Else Know That I Don't? by Michele Novotni (1998). Plantation, FL: Speciality Press Inc.

Self Esteem Bible: Build up your Confidence Day by Day by Gael Lindenfield (2004). London: Element Books. High self-esteem contributes to better communication skills.

See also Chapter 2, p.33 for information about cognitive-behavioural therapy which can also help with communication skills.

Chapter 5

ORGANISING
YOURSELF

Everyday life is a real struggle for people with dyspraxia. The basic stuff – keeping clean and pre-sentable, getting from A to B, cooking and cleaning – is tiring and time-consuming. This chapter, about personal skills you need from day to day, and the next chapter, about organising your home and doing chores, are intended to give you ideas for simplifying living and maybe for starting to tackle seemingly impossible challenges.

Personal care and hygiene
People who have symptoms of dyspraxia, co-ordination difficul-ties and/or perceptuo-motor difficulties need to spend more time and effort than the average person working on their personal appearance, body image and spatial skills.

If you have problems with fine motor skills and with percep-tion, maintaining high standards of grooming and personal hygiene can be difficult.

Dental care
Brushing evenly while moving the toothbrush to reach every surface of the tooth requires great manual dexterity. To brush effectively you could try an electric toothbrush with a timer. You

could also use a mirror to see what you are doing. Dental sticks may be more effective than floss, which has to be manipulated. You can also get attachments to electric toothbrushes to do the flossing.

Visit the dentist and hygienist regularly. They can demonstrate the best methods to clean your teeth and advise on the best equipment.

When undergoing dental examinations or treatment you may gag more than most people. Explaining this to your dentist and asking for the chair to be in a fairly upright position can ease the problem.

Taking medicines

You may be able to get your medication in liquid form if you find swallowing pills difficult. Some tablets must be consumed whole, as the drug in them is released slowly. Place the pill towards the back of your tongue and take three or four gulps of water to get it down. Concentrate on swallowing the water rather than on swallowing the tablet. A capsule is easier to wash down if you put it along your tongue rather than across it.

If you need an inhaler for a condition such as asthma, ask your doctor or pharmacy for an inhaler where you do not have to inhale whilst squeezing it.

Maintaining high standards of grooming and personal hygiene can be difficult

Toileting

Constipation and irritable bowel syndrome can be caused by problems in contracting the abdominal muscles and pushing at the same time. Exercise and eating more fibre can help to alleviate these symptoms (although people with dyspraxia often do not enjoy either physical activities or the chewing needed for fibre). Wet wipes can be easier to use than toilet paper.

Periods

Sanitary towels with wings will probably stick to you rather than their intended position! Towels which have just one self-adhesive strip are probably easier to handle.

Contraception

If you decide to go on the pill, use a timer with a buzzer or talking alarm clock to remind you every day. You might prefer to investigate the option of contraceptive injections which last for several months. Other forms of contraception may prove difficult to use properly.

Washing and styling hair

- Have your hair cut in a way that is easy to manage and needs no styling when washed.

- Before you start, gather together everything you need, including a towel.

- The easiest way to wash your hair is in a stand-up shower, or over the bath using the shower attachment.

Have your hair cut in a way that is easy to manage

- Use plastic containers of shampoo or for rinsing, not glass or china.

Shaving

An electric shaver is easier and safer to use than a manual one. A shaver from the more expensive end of the range, with safety guards will be best.

Makeup

This can be difficult to put on properly. Try to get some free advice from a beauty therapist in your local department store.

- Makeup should always be applied in good light.

- Mirrors on stands or magnified shaving mirrors are useful. Use a hand mirror for applying eye makeup and lipstick.

- Rest your elbow or forearm on a flat surface when applying makeup.

- Always apply a small amount first. If you put on too much it can be very hard to get off.

- Put on foundation first. Use powder rather than liquid, in a colour that is near to your skin tone.

- Soft, matt shades of eyeshadow, such as brown and purple, are more forgiving of smudges and blots than shiny bright blue or green.

- Eyeliner is particularly difficult to apply, so you might want to try going without it.

- A mascara brush with a firm spiralling set of bristles is very effective. Just apply mascara to the tips of your eyelashes. Or do away with mascara altogether and have your lashes dyed.

- The first time you pluck your eyebrows, get someone to do it for you so that you start with two symmetrical brows!

- Apply lipstick with a brush, once the pointed end has worn away for smoother application and greater control.

Colour Me Beautiful by Carolyn Jackson (1984). London: Ballantine Books. A classic on the subject.

> *Even though I have overcome many elements of dyspraxia (I can now use a pair of scissors) I still find many everyday chores incredibly difficult, such as blow-drying my hair and applying makeup.*
>
> Denise

Clothes

Choosing clothes

Its regrettable but true that people meeting you for the first time tend to judge you by your appearance. So looking good can make all the difference to your life.

An image consultant can help you to build up a wardrobe. He or she can tell you what colours are best for you and what shapes of garment will flatter your figure. Alternatively, consult somebody whose fashion sense you admire.

Looking good can make all the difference to your life

For clues on co-ordinating an effective wardrobe, look in stores and shop windows to see displays of items that have already been matched. Some people simplify their dressing by wearing just these items, rather than attempting to mix and match from their own wardrobe.

If you find choosing clothes is stressful, try these ideas:

- Take somebody to help you when you go shopping.

- Restrict the number of shops you visit to a maximum of three.

- Limit the number of garments you try on in each shop, especially if you find dressing and doing up buttons difficult.

- Order clothes by mail. You can try them on in the privacy of your own home.

- Dress parties can be more friendly and relaxed than a shop. Friends at the party can advise you about the clothes.

For clues on co-ordinating an effective wardrobe, look in stores and shop windows

> *I hate clingy clothes and wear everything too big. I am always pulling at the neck of sweaters and at anything near my middle.*
>
> Karen

Colour Me Confident – Change Your Looks – Change Your Style by Veronique Henderson and Pat Henshaw (2006). London: Hamlyn.

www.houseofcolour.co.uk for consultations on image and style for men and women.

Dressing

- If you find fasteners on clothes or jewellery difficult to do up, practise fastening them when the items of clothes or jewellery are not being worn and you can see what you are doing. Then practise fastening them with your eyes shut before you put them on.

- Looking in a mirror can also help you to do up fastenings.

- If doing-up is still difficult, use velcro.

- Establish a dressing routine that becomes automatic.

- Check that your clothes drawers are well organised and labelled.

- Be sure you have chosen the right garment for the occasion.

- When dressing for a special occasion, prepare as much as possible in advance.

- Get up earlier if necessary or decide on your clothes the night before and leave them out. Avoid rushing if possible!

Buy shoes that fit snugly around the heel

The inability to tie bows still haunts me!

Clare

Footwear

- Avoid high heels, especially narrow ones as they are very difficult to balance on.

- Thick soles or platform shoes are not a good idea – you need to have some sensation of the ground underneath your feet. If the soles of your shoes are heavy you are more likely to trip up and twist your ankle.

- Shoes which have welt on the sole sticking out at the front can make you trip.

- Buy shoes that fit snugly around the heel and do not slip forward.

- Avoid shoes with slippery soles. Try to buy pairs with rubber soles which will not skid on wet or shiny floors.

Spectacles

Make sure that your specs sit comfortably. The tiny screws that hold the arms on often work loose after prolonged wear. If the specs become uncomfortable, the ear pieces can be adjusted to lengthen the arms.

Umbrellas

Forget about umbrellas altogether. If you don't leave your brolly on a bus, you will probably prod someone when you put it up. Remember the nightmare of walking along a crowded street on a windy day, talking to someone and holding up your umbrella. A raincoat with a hood is much easier to deal with.

The Disability Living Foundation produces lots of factsheets about dressing, clothes, footwear and eating and drinking, etc.
380–384 Harrow Road, London W9 2HU. Tel: 0845 130917, www.dlf.org.uk

Budgeting and shopping

Many people with dyspraxia find the details of budgeting and saving very dull. We are often impulsive and buy things on a whim.

Keeping till receipts and doing bookkeeping is a chore. Computer programs such as Quicken can help with keeping records, although cheap programs can be limited in their layout options. Your local Citizens Advice Bureau can provide advice on budgeting and debt management.

Debtors Anonymous UK (with meetings all over the country).
Tel: 020 7644 5070, www.debtorsanonymous.org.uk.

National Debtline. Tel: 0808 808 4000, www.nationaldebtline.co.uk. For lots of free information to download on budgeting, etc.

Solutions for Specific Learning Difficulties – Identification Guide by Jan Poustie (1997). Taunton: Next Generation.

Life Skills: Practical Solutions for Specific Learning Difficulties by Jan Poustie (1998). Taunton: Next Generation. Good also for organising your home – see the next chapter.

The Money Diet Book by Martin Lewis (2004). London: Vermilion.

How to Get Out of Debt, Stay Out of Debt and Live Prosperously (Based on Proven Principles and Techniques at Debtors Anonymous) by Jerrold Mundis (1990). London: Bantam Books.

Dyscalculia – difficulty with numbers – affects budgeting and shopping. It can be hard to find the right money and to check change quickly. A transparent purse enables you to see what coins you have when you reach the checkout.

Many stores now run telephone and internet shopping services. These suit people with dyspraxia. You can choose your shopping in the quiet of your own home, in your own time. The to-your-door delivery service is ideal for those who cannot drive.

Keep a template for regular shopping (see details under Plan your chores, p.77).

We are often impulsive and buy things on a whim

> If I can get through a week without losing a purse or a bag, then I am very proud of myself. My husband has to go to the supermarket with me. Now automatically when I have paid for the shopping he takes my purse off me and gives it back when we get home. Shopkeepers are used to me in particular shops. They remind me to pick up my shopping and put my purse away. It's so humiliating, I just want to blend into the floor. I hate myself at these times. My family laugh and joke about it all the time. I do laugh with them, but it still hurts.
>
> Karen

Written presentation

When you leave school or college you probably will not need to produce large amounts of handwritten work. Instead, you will probably use a computer. However, personal letters and application forms are still sometimes written by hand, so legible, well-set-out handwriting is still useful. Handwriting will be easier if you use appropriate equipment and sit in the right way.

Improve your handwriting

- First, choose your pen or pencil. There are many different types on the market which have grips that help you write better and more easily. Pens with fibre tips or rollerballs exert friction and are easier to control than ballpoints. Liquid ink rollerball pens are very responsive and are available from most stationery shops. Hard, sharp pencils are useful for precision.

- Sit on a chair which is well pulled up to the table.

- The chair should be high enough that your forearms rest comfortably on the table.

Personal letters and application forms are often written by hand

- The chair should give good support along your thigh but the seat should not dig into the back of your knee.

- Your feet should be able to rest flat on the floor. If they can't, rest your feet on a small stool or box.

- If you are right-handed, position the bottom left-hand corner of the paper in line with the middle of your body. Rotate the paper 15–20 degrees anticlockwise.

- If you are left-handed, position the bottom right hand corner of the paper in line with the middle of your body. Rotate the paper about 25 degrees clockwise. The extra rotation of the paper lets you see the current line of writing.

- Your non-writing hand should support the top of the writing paper.

Word processing

When you use a keyboard for the first time, you will long to write by hand instead! Before long, word processing will be less effort than holding a pen and of course will be easier to read than handwriting. Your writing will also be infinitely editable, so that the completed work will be pleasing to the reader and satisfying to you, the writer.

Whichever word processing programme you use, you will need to learn keyboard skills – the position of each letter on the board and the use of each finger. Very short and frequent practice sessions are usually the most effective. It may be easier to learn using a book rather than a computer program, which often requires speed and perfection before you are allowed to progress to the next stage. However, many learner typists swear by the Mavis Beacon software, which is available in versions suitable for both children and adults.

Keyboarding Skills for Children with Disabilities by Dorothy Penso (1999). London: Whurr.

Mavis Beacon Teaches Typing Deluxe V17 (2001). San Francisco, CA: Riverdeep.

i There are also typing courses especially for people with dyspraxia and dyslexia in some parts of the country. Ring the helpline 020 7545 7891 for more details. See also Chapter 7, under Technology can help (p.105).

> **Before long, word processing will be less effort than holding a pen**

Eating, drinking and parties

Eating out and going to pubs can be stressful as well as enjoyable. Many of us are messy eaters who spill food and drink down ourselves. At buffet parties it can be almost impossible to hold a plate, a fork and a drink at the same time. Standing by the table with food and eating with your fingers and no plate can avoid accidents; but sitting in a chair makes the whole balancing act much easier and more comfortable.

Preventing the messy table

- To minimise the distance you need to transport food between plate and mouth, tuck your chair as far as possible under the dining table. Sit straight with your body against the edge of the table and your feet flat on the floor.

- Use your napkin to keep your clothes clean – tucked into your top or on your lap.

- Ensure that wine glasses, tumblers and cups are not over-full.

- Ask for salt, water, etc. to be passed to you rather than reaching across the table for them.

- Concentrate hard when cutting to stop food sliding from the plate to the table.

- Cut up over-large pieces of food.

- Choose food that is easy to eat. A slice or fillet of meat is easier to cut than meat on the bone.

Travelling really can be a nightmare

- If you are eating at home, special cutlery and plates can help to prevent spillages. These are available from the Disabled Living Foundation – see p.87 for details.

- Practise eating spaghetti and noodles at home!

Travelling

Travelling really can be a nightmare. Just crossing the road can be a problem, because of difficulties with concentration and in judging distance and speed. Catching buses, coaches and trains is a strain too. A poor sense of direction may mean that you take a long while to find the right boarding place or platform. Lack of sense of time and difficulty with concentrating on and tracking lines of timetables may mean you end up at the wrong place at the wrong time.

One solution may be…

Cycling

Riding a bike improves road sense and distance judgement and can be good preparation for learning to drive a car. However, difficulties with balance and co-ordination can mean cycling is almost impossible.

- Choose an old-fashioned bike with straight handlebars, rather than a sporting bike, to give you a sense of stability and security.

- The saddle should be low enough for the soles of your feet to be firmly on the ground when you stand astride the bike. Any higher, and you may not feel secure.

- Mirrors on your handlebars enable you to see vehicles which are about to overtake you.

- If you live in a flat area and have the thigh muscles to cope, ride a tricycle. Everyone else on the road will avoid you!

Riding a bike improves road sense and distance judgement

Driving

To be able to concentrate, steer, judge distance, use both hands and feet together and remember how to carry out a sequence of tasks all at the same time is something that many people with dyspraxia find daunting. It is hardly surprising that a lot of us decide that driving a car is beyond our capabilities. However, social pressures and work commitments may compel us to at least give driving a try.

Only you know what your difficulties are

> *It took me forever to learn to drive a car. I lost count of the number of lessons, but it took six tests.*
>
> Louise

Facilities for learner drivers with co-ordination difficulties have improved greatly over the past few years. A number of assessment centres throughout the country now offer information and advice to drivers who have a disability and assess them in a safe environment to establish their capabilities.

Details of your nearest centre are available from the Department of Transport's Mobility Advice and Vehicle Information Service (MAVIS). The staff at MAVIS are very helpful and are used to working with people with poor concentration and perceptual and spatial awareness problems

 MAVIS. Tel: 01344 661000, www.dft.gov.uk/access/mavis. For information about concessions on the theory test contact Drive Safe, the special needs team at the Driving Standards Agency. Tel: 0870 01013721.

The British School of Motoring offers a range of courses which cater for specialist needs. Some of their branches have driving simulators, with geared cars, to build your confidence before you take to the open road.

If you decide to use a local driving school, shop around and ask questions. Only you know what your difficulties are. It is up to you to make a prospective instructor aware of them.

You may be able to track down an instructor who has taught people with disabilities, who is patient and has the experience to teach techniques that will help you to learn.

DRIVING TIPS

- Try to learn in an automatic car. There are fewer co-ordination tasks and less to think about.

- When taking the test, ask for extra time to complete the written section if you think you need it.

- Have extra wing mirrors fitted for easier parking and reversing.

- Larger, higher-mounted steering wheels are easier to use.

- Mark the right side of the steering wheel with a sticker to help you to remember which side is right and which is left.

- Plan and prepare your journey as much as possible before you set out. Write down the directions and clip them to the dashboard or buy a satellite navigation system.

- If you have map-reading problems, upside down maps can help.

- Take frequent breaks if you find concentration difficult.

Not-driving is the last great taboo. In mad moments I long for a wooden leg to wave, like Long John Silver: This is why I don't drive, OK?

Jenny

Chapter 6

ORGANISING YOUR HOME

If you have dyspraxia, it takes constant effort to keep your home clean and tidy and to co-operate with others who live with you.

People who do not have dyspraxia often do not understand that it can be particularly hard to manage the time available for household chores, to organise a task and to work methodically through it.

This chapter aims to help you to plan and to make your daily life at home that little bit easier.

> *I try to tidy up all the time, but the house always looks a mess. I'm never on top of it.*
>
> Lucy

Organising your time

Time management sounds boring, but the more you organise your time the more you will get done. Time spent planning each day really can help you to achieve what you need to do.

Plan your chores

You might want to try out these ideas to make the best use of your time.

- Take a few minutes at the beginning of each day to plan what you are doing.

- Set yourself clearly defined goals. Then break down into manageable steps the tasks you need to complete to achieve those goals.

- Give yourself firm time boundaries to complete tasks.

- Put up a weekly or monthly planner or calendar in a prominent position – on the back of the kitchen door, or on the fridge. Mark on it any appointments and any jobs you have to do on a particular day.

- Use the planner/calendar to note down chores like cleaning the fridge, degreasing the oven and cleaning certain rooms. You could even allocate particular times to do the jobs. That way, the less pleasant household tasks get done on a regular basis.

The more you organise your time the more you will get done

- Stick up Post-It notes in obvious places to help you remember things you might forget.

- Get a large diary with a whole page for each day. At the beginning of each day, write down everything you plan to do. If you prefer, use an electronic planner which will 'beep' when you need to do particular things.

- Always prioritise tasks into those you have to do and those that can be left for another day. Colour coding the different types of tasks – letters to write, bills to pay, telephone calls to make, items to buy – may make time planning easier.

- Allocate a specific time to do each job.

- Establish a routine or a sequence for tasks you hate doing. If you develop a habit of doing automatically a job such as tidying up, you won't feel 'quite right' until you have done it.

- 'Piggyback' actions to help you to remember them. 'When I have brushed my teeth I will take my pills.'

- Try to get somebody to make sure that you stick to what you say you will do, in a constructive and supportive way.

- Make a template shopping list for items bought regularly like bread and milk, and add additional items that you need that day.

 Successful Time Management in a Week by Declan Treacy Ltd (1998). London: Hodder Stoughton.

Planning the big jobs

You need to build in time for relaxation

Long and complicated jobs, such as cleaning the kitchen, arranging to go away, de-cluttering your home in preparation for a visit, or sorting out your paperwork, need strategic planning. You need to build in time for relaxation.

- Plan the job by breaking it down into small segments. Build in the time for frequent rests.

- Set realistic start and stop times for each action. A project which has a defined end is much less daunting than one that seems endless.

- Use a kitchen timer with an alarm. Give yourself permission to stop after the time you have set yourself for a particular task.

- Identify any blocks or resistances you have to certain tasks or projects. Sort them out before they sabotage the job.

- Mind maps (see Chapter 7 for details) can help you to plan difficult jobs.

- Establish markers to identify the completion of each stage of a project – 'When I've finished labelling my files, I've done the second step of the job.'

- Give yourself a reward when you have completed a task that you particularly hate doing.

Clearing the clutter

Although people with dyspraxia have difficulties with organising themselves and their environment, time and effort spent in organising your home and keeping it in order will be very worthwhile.

Having a living space that is tidy and well organised makes every aspect of life so much easier and can reduce your stress levels.

If you break down de-cluttering into small tasks, you really can be neat and have a place for everything.

De-junking

- If something is broken, torn or unsafe to use, throw it away or recycle it.

When you finish de-cluttering, the cleaning can begin

- If an item has not been used in the past two years consider donating it to a charity shop. If it could be useful in the future, store it separately from things which are in regular use. Of course, you might suddenly find a use for it right now!

- Keep 'like' things together in the same place – in a box or cupboard, or on a shelf. Everything should have its place!

- Find a special place to keep important items that you keep losing, such as keys and glasses. Put these away in their correct place as soon as you have finished using them.

- Keep all tools, such as hammers and screwdrivers, in the same box labelled 'tools'. Put screws, nails and picture hooks with them.

- Most people need a needle and thread at some time, and it is all too easy to leave needles lying about. Have a box labelled 'sewing' for needles, pins, thread and scissors.

De-clutter your rooms

IN THE KITCHEN

- Invest in a purpose-made box to keep cutlery, particularly sharp knives, in separate compartments.

- Larders and fridges can fill up with groceries that are rarely used and food that has passed its 'use by' date. Sort through your cupboards and fridge on a regular basis, so that mess and muddle is less likely and you do not end up eating food which is past its best.

- When clearing the larder put all similar items, such as herbs, together in a box.

- If you need to keep your shelves cleaned regularly, make a chart inside the cupboard doors or on the side of the fridge. Tick off against the chart and date it when the clear-out has been completed.

If the household chores really become too much, try to find a cleaner

IN THE BATHROOM

- Keep all toiletries out of sight in cupboards or in drawers. Label shelves and drawers with the items they are intended to contain. If you do not have enough cupboards or drawers, invest in some plastic baskets so that you can clear surfaces of bottles, bits and bobs easily for cleaning.

IN THE BEDROOM

- Coat hangers are cheap, so buy enough to hang up each garment separately. You will then be able to view your wardrobe at a glance.

IN THE LIVING ROOM

- 'Minimalism' is probably the best style for you! The fewer ornaments, mats and pictures you have on display, the easier cleaning will be and the tidier and more attractive the room will look.

 www.flylady.com. A site you can join and which sends out daily reminders of how and when to organise your home, and de-clutter.

Cleaning up

When you finish de-cluttering, the cleaning can begin.

- Clear the whole surface before you attempt to clean it. This is a much more efficient way of cleaning than moving objects one by one.

- Work systematically over the whole surface so that you don't have to come back later to clean the parts you have missed.

- A damp duster is more effective than a dry one. You can spray polish directly onto the duster.

- To minimise dusting, try reducing the number of ornaments you have on display.

- To clean a sink, fill the sink with hot water and then just pour in bleach or washing powder and leave it for 10 to 15 minutes. This really cleans and shines the sink without much effort.

- Antibacterial wipes are wonderful as they clean and dry at the same time – and then you throw them away. These are particularly good for cleaning dirty toilet seats and for disposing of cat mess.

SOME USEFUL CLEANING TOOLS

- A 'wet and dry' cylinder vacuum cleaner will suck up mess on the kitchen floor.

- A dustpan with a long handle is often easier to use than the traditional type.

- Dusters and cloths. You will get through a lot when you are damp dusting (see above) and you may find washing the kitchen floor easier with a floor cloth than with a mop. You can clean around the edges of kitchen units better on your hands and knees with a cloth!

VACUUMING

You may find controlling a vacuum cleaner difficult and bump the machine into furniture. Try out the different types of cleaner before you decide which to buy.

- Upright vacuum cleaners can be difficult to use on stairs and cumbersome to carry up and down. Cylinder cleaners are probably better than uprights.

- A model with a 'beep' or light which indicates when the dust bag is full can be helpful. Of course, you could always choose a cleaner without a dust bag.

- Cleaners with an automatically rewinding flex are easy and quick to use and to put away. You are less likely to trip over the flex if you feed the surplus back into the machine.

Plan your cooking to use the minimum number of pans

If the household chores really become too much, arrange for a cleaner to come in occasionally to help you. You may be able to get a cleaner through your social services department if your dyspraxia is severe enough and if you are prepared to be very persistent.

Washing dishes and clothes

Washing dishes and clothes can be very tiresome and very wet when water pours over the edge of the sink, down your clothes and onto the floor. Dishwashers and washing machines are probably the ideal solutions, but can't always be used by everybody.

> *Before I had a dishwasher people used to think I had put my glasses away dirty!*
>
> Mary

- The larger the bowl, the easier and drier washing-up will be. Items can be drained on the drainer instead of dried with a tea-towel. Draining saves time and is more hygienic.

- A rolled-up towel laid around the edges of the sink can act as a dam to catch most of the water.

- Plan your cooking to use the minimum number of pans. There will be less washing-up and less mess.

- Use non-stick pans which are easier to wash than ordinary ones.

- To minimise cleaning, line the bottom of the oven, your grill and your ovenware with aluminium foil.

Machine washing and ironing

Household chores take forever. It usually takes me about three-quarters of an hour to iron a blouse.

Louise

- Choose clothes and bedlinen which need the minimum of ironing, without pleats and frills.

- Patterned clothes mask stains better than plain ones and will consequently need less washing. Think hard before you buy anything white!

- Avoid clothes that need dry-cleaning, as this can be very expensive.

- Sort your washing first in to coloured and white to make sure that colours do not run.

- Refer to the labels on your clothes and choose the correct washing and spin-drying cycle for the most delicate item in that wash.

- Don't overload the machine – if you do it may overflow. If necessary, weigh the load on the bathroom scales.

- Washing machine nets keep small items together. Sock clips can be used to pair your socks.

- After washing, tumble-dry clothes for five minutes and put them on clothes hangers. Even if you do not use a tumble-dryer, garments hung on hangers will dry with few creases and no peg marks. Clothes on hangers are easy to take down from the line and quick to put back in the wardrobe – useful if you have a weak shoulder girdle and find that raising your arms is tiring.

- Cordless irons and ironing boards which are wall-mounted or rest on table tops are safer and more straightforward than traditional models.

Cooking

Try cooking easy things first and progress to complicated recipes later

Those with co-ordination and spatial difficulties tend to spill and drop things more often than most. They may also burn food as they find it hard to concentrate and are easily distracted. The kitchen, with its hot liquids, fats and foods is particularly hazardous and is a source of distractions, because it is usually a focal point for everyone in the household.

It is a good idea to try cooking easy things first and progress to complicated recipes later. After all, simple cooking is good cooking!

Kitchen design

- There should be heatproof surfaces next to the cooker and microwave for hot pans and plates.

- Arrange your kitchen equipment so that there is no need to reach across your cooker or across hot kettles or pans.

- Turn saucepan handles away from the edge of the cooker or hob.

- Knives are less likely to cause accidental injury if they are kept in a special place. Store them separately from other equipment.

- Label drawers and cupboards to help you find things.

> *I used to keep sharp knives in the drawer with other implements like the tin opener and the corkscrew. I was often in a panic to find these and jabbed myself several times.*
>
> Mary

Ovens

- Oven and microwave cooking tends to be easier and less dangerous than frying and grilling. You are less likely to burn food in an oven. You also have to handle baked or roasted food less frequently than grilled or fried. Most ovens have timers which ring when the food has been cooked for the set time.

- Electric ovens are simpler to light than gas ovens, especially if the model has controls which are easy to manipulate. Electric hobs are also quicker to clean than gas hobs. However, heat on an electric ring is harder to control – how often have you put a pan of water on to boil and switched on the wrong electric ring?

- Microwaves stop automatically. They remain cool while they are in operation; and they cook quickly, which means you spend little time in the kitchen. Food can be cooked in its serving dish, so that you save time washing up too. The microwave itself is easy to clean because food does not get burned onto its surface.

Digital kitchen timer

Useful kitchen equipment

- A **toaster** – easier and cheaper to use than the grill

- A **portable kitchen timer**, digital or analogue – the larger and louder the better

---

*   Reproduced by kind permission of the Disabled Living Foundation

- **Tongs** to turn items on the grill or in the frying pan – safer than forks or spatulas

- A **colander** to drain vegetables, as opposed to using the saucepan lid

- A **mesh basket or sieve** to cook vegetables inside the saucepan – you can lift the vegetables out all together and the water will drain straight back into the pan, which does not need to be moved

- A **pair of oven gloves** joined together – safer for handling hot food than a single oven mitt

- A **cordless kettle** that lights up when you switch it on and shows how much water it contains – switching on an empty kettle can have explosive consequences!

- A **kettle tipper** that means you do not have to lift the kettle to pour out the boiling liquid – you must make sure that you get the right design of tipper for your kettle

Kettle tipper

- A **chopping board** with spikes and clamps to fix food firmly while you peel and chop it, some also have plastic suction feet that stick to the work surface – you could also put an ordinary chopping board on a non-slip plastic mat

- **Digital or talking scales**

- A **tin opener** which suits you – some people with dyspraxia are devoted to their electric tin opener; others find manual ones better

Cone-shaped plastic jar opener

- A **carton opener** – again, try as many as you can before you buy

- A **cone-shaped plastic jar opener** provides extra leverage and cuts down on the effort of twisting and pulling.

*   Reproduced by kind permission of the Disabled Living Foundation

Preparing food

- Make sure your chopping board is stable and secure before you start (see above).

- There are many gadgets available which help you to slice or chop different types of food, such as bread, eggs, or tomatoes. A spring-loaded chopper is relatively safe as its blades are hidden inside the plastic container. You could try using a knife with a circular blade to chop up herbs.

- Electric and manual food processors chop, slice and blend, although they can take a long time to dismantle, clean and reassemble and have sharp parts.

- For control when cutting and slicing, use scissors (especially the self-opening type) rather than knives. Knives should be kept as sharp as possible so that they are easy to use.

- For peeling, grating and mashing, it is best to experiment with several different designs of utensil to see which suits you best.

Get out everything you will need before starting to cook

Following a recipe

Rewrite the recipe in small simple stages, including every single process and detail. For example: 'Get the following ingredients out...chop them up and put them in separate bowls...'. Leave nothing to the memory or imagination, however obvious the instructions may seem. It is a good idea to get out everything you will need before starting to cook as this will help you to get everything ready to be served at the same time.

i You could start by looking through household gadgets catalogues such as Betterware and Kleeneze which offer useful implements at reasonable prices. Boots stores provide mail order catalogues of helpful gadgets. Some bigger branches sell these items direct.

Disabled Living Foundation. Tel: 0845 130 9177 (helpline), www.dlf.org.uk. There are Disability Centres all over the country where you can try out gadgets and equipment free of charge. A list of the gadgets and equipment and details of where you can buy them are available via the helpline.

The Dyscovery Shop at the Dyscovery Centre, University of Wales, Newport Allt–Yn campus, Newport, NP20 5DA. Tel: 01633 432 330, www.dyscovery.co.uk. Sells a range of useful equipment including kettle tippers, electric hand-held tin openers and a 'vegetable workstation' for peeling potatoes and carrots with one hand.

Nottingham Rehab, Findell House, Excelsior Road, Ashby-de-la-Zouch, Leicestershire LE65 1NG. Tel: 0845 606 0911, www.nrs-uk.co.uk. Publish a large catalogue full of aids for daily living.

Peta (Toolcraft) Ltd, Mark's Hall, Mark's Hall Lane, Margaret Roding, Essex CM6 1QT. Tel: 01245 231118, www.peta-uk.com. Publish catalogues of ergonomically designed garden tools and palmar grip scissors.

Choosing Household Equipment. DLF Factsheet (2006) Disability Living Foundation. Tel: 0845 130 9177, www.dlf.org.uk.

Perceptuo-Motor Difficulties by Dorothy Penso (1993). London: Chapman and Hall.

Scissors Skills by Dorothy Penso (2004). London: Whurr.

Self-opening scissors – useful for craftwork

Sewing and craftwork

- A high proportion of people with co-ordination problems are left-handed. As they will have discovered, most tools are designed for the right-handed person. Left-handers may find that it is worth investing in tools such as scissors which are specially designed for them.

- Scissors come in many designs, including those for people with poor grip and poor rhythmic movements. Some whole-hand grip scissors have springs which makes cutting easier to control. You can find out which scissors are best for different jobs at a Disability Centre (see above).

*   Reproduced by kind permission of the Disabled Living Foundation

- Intricate curves and shapes can be particularly demanding to cut. Your scissors should enable you to make very small cuts, synchronised with the small adjustments of the material in the other hand.

- If you need to cut a straight line, use a ruler to draw the line and cut along it.

Sewing

If you have problems with sequencing and with short-term memory, threading up a sewing machine and following the instructions can be hard. Dorothy Penso's book (see above) gives advice on using sewing machines.

A self-threading needle is what you need for sewing tasks such as stitching on a button. Of course, it is possible to avoid sewing completely. You can hem clothes and repair tears using iron-on materials. Many dry cleaners offer alteration and repair services.

You may be able to try out different types of tools at a Disability Centre

Do-it-yourself

There are no easy answers – DIY can be really difficult. Putting up wallpaper, along with carpentry, plumbing and electrical work are best left to the experts. Try reading the leaflets and basic guides to these skills that are available in DIY stores. Watching DIY videos over and over again may help you to do the job.

Paint pads are easy to use and make less mess than brushes. Wear a paint overall and have a damp rag beside you all the time to wipe up drops immediately.

Gardening

People with dyspraxia can find it difficult to use gardening tools. You may be able to try out different types of tools at a Disability Centre. Gardening videos may help you to get the knack of using the implements and of the different digging and planting techniques.

Dyspraxic adults may never master skills requiring co-ordination such as performing simple DIY jobs, repairing or mending things, because they may be unable to use tools or implements. They are thus unable to perform many simple and basic tasks that most people take for granted and may be forced to pay for simple jobs to be done.

Shirley

Chapter 7

Studying
with Dyspraxia

Whether you hope to go to college or university straight after school or plan to start studies after a long break, the difficulties you may well have encountered at school are likely to continue – as are the strengths you will have developed to counteract your dyspraxia, such as creativity and lateral thinking. Some students with dyspraxia have few problems with course work or exams but can find practical tasks very difficult. These might include:

Manual and practical work

- Problems using computer keyboards
- Frequent spills in the laboratory
- Lack of organisation in experiments
- Difficulty measuring accurately
- Slow and illegible handwriting
- Messy presentation.

Personal presentation

- Untidy and rumpled
- Poor posture
- Frequently bumping into things and tripping over.

Written expression

- Erratic spelling and punctuation
- Awkward and confused sentence structure
- Poor proofreading
- Slow to complete examinations.

Work organisation

- Poor at taking notes, especially copying figures
- Disorganised and repetitive essays
- Inclusion of irrelevant material in written work
- Slow to make use of new vocabulary
- Cluttered working area.

Personal organisation

- Tendency to be chaotic, forgetful and disorganised
- Poor at time-keeping: missed appointments (often because of misread notices).

Memory and attention span

- Short attention span
- Poor short-term memory
- Easily distracted, particularly by noise and bright light
- Difficulty in following group discussions
- Slow retrieval of information, especially when under stress
- Slow to tackle reading lists because of inability to 'skim read'
- Trouble keeping place in books and written exercises
- Tendency to become disorientated and get lost in college buildings.

Visual skills

- Trouble in keeping place when reading
- Difficultly with copying from a blackboard or similar.

Oral skills

- Difficulty with word-finding
- Wrong pronunciation of newly introduced words
- Speaking indistinctly, loudly, fast
- Interrupting inappropriately
- Difficulty in learning foreign languages.

Numeracy skills

- Tendency to reverse and mis-copy numbers, signs and decimal points
- Frequent, apparently careless errors.

Most students with dyspraxia suffer at some stage from anxiety, stress, low self-esteem and depression because of the multiple difficulties they experience. I did not suffer academically, as I gained a degree without too much difficulty. But I have lived very much 'in my head' with little faith or confidence in my body. I always played up to this uselessness – pointing out my shortcomings before others could – and this led others to view me as severely as I did myself.

Ceri

Choosing the right course and the right college for you is very important

Finding the right place

Choosing the right course and the right college for you is very important, not just for your future but for your wellbeing while you are studying. Find out as much as possible about the course before you apply.

You might want to ask the college and yourself the following:

- How much support is there for people with specific learning difficulties? There is no doubt that some colleges provide better support than others.
- How much practical work is there?
- How much writing will there be?
- How much support will you get?

- Will the course involve working with numbers?
- Will you be assessed mainly on course work or through examinations?
- Will you have to do work experience? Less support is provided there than in college.
- What grants are available? (See pp.95–96)
- Will you be able to cope away from home?
- Can you live in a hall of residence where meals are provided?
- Do you know anybody who could share a flat?

Get full details of the support which is available

In the Upper Sixth, my history teacher wanted me to take the Oxford entrance exam. This was not because of academic excellence but because she said that I had an original mind. In fact this meant that I often got hold of the wrong end of the stick in exams and could find ambiguities where no one else could.

I passed the exam and was called for interview. At this point I lost my confidence. I felt that it was all a big mistake.

I was sure that the clever people at Oxford would spot the stupidity that I had learned so well to hide. I ended up by achieving an A and twos Bs in my A-levels. Mum was so overcome that she cried and I went off to study history at Southampton University.

Heather

Visits and interviews

Most colleges run open days for prospective students. These are excellent opportunities to familiarise yourself with the facilities and to get full details of the support which is available, such as study-skills classes and self-help groups. See 'What help will you need at college?' below for ideas on issues to raise. You might also want to read the 'Interviews' section in Chapter 8.

Your local Connexions or Careers Service may be able to help you to decide on what course would be best for you.

If you left school with no qualifications, you can attend courses which are aimed at encouraging independence and developing social skills. Other courses are more vocational. You may be able to attend a specialist residential college, if you need to learn daily living skills. These colleges have more appropriate equipment than the average further education college.

> **i** www.after16.org.uk is a very useful website that gives information about all options including education, for young people with hdisabilities and learning difficulties, and lists college courses.
>
> *AchieveAbility – SpLD the Way Forward*: A CD Rom ro guide students with specific learning differences into university. See www.achieveability.org.uk for more information about this project. You can also contact Skill – see below for details.

> *I had been so frustrated. I could only get menial jobs doing physical work, which is the hardest for me to do because of my disability. I decided to go back to college and get qualifications so that I could get a job that uses my brain.*
>
> Colin

Disabled Students Allowance

In England, students who have dyspraxia and who have been accepted on a course of full-time, part-time, or distance higher or post-graduate education (not further education) can apply for the Disabled Students Allowance (DSA) from their local education authority (LEA). This is also true of the Open University.

The DSA covers wages for non-medical personal helpers, such as extra tutorial help or note-takers; and special equipment such as computers. You may also claim for photocopying and a book allowance.

To claim the DSA you need to have had a recent assessment, usually by an educational psychologist. The report from this should be sent to the university and LEA, once you've been offered a conditional place. Your LEA will ask you to have a needs assessment carried out to identify your exact needs.

The college's Welfare Officer or the Disabled Students Adviser may be able to help you with your claim and supply you with more information, as can the LEA officer for DSA.

Students who are in further education cannot claim DSA. However, an access grant may be available from your college, which is likely to have a fund for students in difficulties.

Students can claim a loan of up to £3000 for tuition fees from their local authority in England, which will be paid direct to the university. In Scotland, tuition fees, in most cases, are paid for by the Scottish Awards Agency for Scotland (SAAS). Students from low-income households will be eligible for a new maintenance grant of up to £2700 in 2006. Others can get loans (or a combination of a loan and a bursary) which have to be paid back when they are earning £15,000 a year. The rules which govern funding in further and higher education are changing constantly. Consult your LEA for up-to-date information.

Students with dyspraxia need sources of regular relaxation

Skill: National Bureau for Students with Disabilities, 3rd Floor Chapter House, 18–20 Crucifix Lane, London SE1 3JW. Tel: 0800 328 5050, www.skill.org.uk. Skill is a specialist organisation which can provide up-to-date information on grants and funding and is a source of extremely useful publications.

Bridging the Gap: A Guide to Disabled Students Allowances (DSAs) in Higher Education DfES

A Guide to Financial Support for Higher Education Students DfES Tel: 0800 731 9133, www.dfes.gov.uk.

Getting started – How your college might help

When you first arrive at college, settling in, finding your way around, setting up routines and meeting many new people will be stressful. Halls of residence may also be very noisy places! Students with dyspraxia are in particular need of sources of regular relaxation and of counselling, so check out classes and societies to do with hobbies, and build these into your new life as well as finding out about sources of support.

Dyspraxic students living away from home are also likely to experience great difficulty with practical things such as cooking and laundry.

I had no problems getting a place at university and was really excited to be starting a degree in modern languages at Exeter. But as soon as I got on campus, everything started to go wrong. It was the practical things which challenged me: close to tears, I'd spend an hour trying to get the key in the door to my student digs. I couldn't find my way around campus and it was a nightmare trying to work out how to use the washing machine or change the duvet on my bed. All of these simple tasks were a massive challenge, but I felt ashamed and so tried to hide my problems from the other students. I couldn't even open a bottle of wine or make someone a cup of tea as it would take me so long.

Nicky

As soon as you can, make an appointment with the Disability Officer or Dyslexia Support Tutor in the Learning Support Centre or Special Needs Department. They will be able to help you with the best ways to approach your tutors about your dyspraxia. They will also be able to tell you about any support or self-help groups; and if there is a 'buddy network' of other students, who could perhaps take notes for you and help with proofreading.

The Disability Officer or Dyslexia Support Tutor will probably tell you about study-skills classes. If they do not, ask them what is available to help students with specific learning disabilities to organise their work, take notes and write essays.

If you have not yet been assessed as having dyspraxia, ask about getting your areas of difficulty highlighted, ideally by an educational psychologist, as the department will probably be able to arrange and pay for it.

Sometimes a teacher with training in specific learning disabilities will be able to assess you, using standard tests. The teacher is likely to take a case history, and give you reading, comprehension, spelling and writing tests similar to those used for testing dyslexia. He or she may also look at the learning demands of your course and recommend any modifications. The reports and recommendations should be circulated to all those who are concerned with your learning and welfare at college.

The tests used for dyspraxia assessment by teachers/tutors include Gardeners TMVS(UL) and the WRIT. The diamonds subtest of the latter is particularly useful in testing for dyspraxia. See p.143 for more details.

As well as letting you claim the allowance to which you will be entitled, assessment and diagnosis of your dyspraxia can help you in other ways. You will be able to understand previous learning failure, and to identify your pattern of strengths and weaknesses in learning.

In September 2002, the Disability Discrimination Act was extended to cover education, making it unlawful for education and training providers to discriminate against disabled people.

Examinations

One of the most important reasons to be assessed for dyspraxia at college is that if you are diagnosed you should be entitled to receive concessions during examinations.

These examination provisions allow students with dyspraxia and/or dyslexia to complete their course on equal terms with other students:

If you are diagnosed for dyspraxia you may receive concessions during examinations

- Extra time for writing and checking work

- Use of a word processor and other technology if the student has great difficulties with longhand writing

- Dictation of answers to an amanuensis or scribe – very helpful for the dyspraxic student who has difficulty in writing quickly under exam conditions

- Oral, rather than written examinations

- Consideration for spelling and organisational difficulties

- A separate room in which to take examinations.

Counselling and pastoral care

College counsellors can usually help you to come to terms with the results of an assessment, to talk through past experiences and to plan the way forward emotionally and socially.

If you find you tend to be too aggressive or too passive, assertiveness training can help you to ask for what you want effectively without alienating people, or being ignored.

If the college does not run these kinds of ancillary support, you can ask about other providers. You can also seek out advice from your tutors on prioritising your work, and from others on establishing a reminder system for lectures and essay deadlines.

Support groups

Feeling that you are suffering in isolation will make you miserable and your academic and social life will be affected.

There is always strength in numbers. Ask the Disability Officer whether there is a support or self-help group that you can join. Alternatively, post a note on a noticeboard or on the internal e-mail system. There are often groups for dyslexics which dyspraxics can join. The Dyslexia Support Tutor, if there is one, should be a source of help as dyslexic and dyspraxic students tend to have similar needs in relation to non-practical subjects.

Getting together with others in the same boat and discussing ways that you can be helped could be the key to ensuring that the college is aware of the practical needs of people with dyspraxia.

In an ideal world, your college should have a policy on helping their students who have dyspraxia, integrated with policies on students with dyslexia and other disabilities; and a commitment to identifying dyspraxia through screening.

All staff should be aware of the condition

All staff should be aware of the condition and either be trained to help students themselves, or know where to refer students. Careers advisers should be experienced in helping those with specific learning disabilities. The college's admissions policy should not discriminate against those with dyspraxia or other learning difficulties.

In an ideal world your college should have a policy on helping their students who have dyspraxia

I studied philosophy and politics at university. My first term in particular was difficult because of repressed memories rising up of my first times away from home when I was five and six.

In my third and final year I befriended several people through my involvement in the Philosophy Society and the Undergraduate Philosophy Conference. I had previously doubted my ability to attain higher than a Lower Second-class degree. Getting to know the people I did, I managed an Upper Second. What they did was to give my self-belief a boost, often unknowingly.

Ben

What help will you need at college?

Approaching individual tutors and lecturers to ask for help because of your condition can be very daunting.

DANDA is indebted to Melanie Jameson, a teacher who specialises in specific learning difficulties in further and higher education, for the following the following ideas of the kinds of assistance you might want to request.

DAY TO DAY

- Acknowledgement that you have a specific learning difficulty.

AT LECTURES AND SEMINARS

- Handouts which include a clear outline of the lecture/subjects to be covered
- Handout presentation to be well spaced and uncluttered
- Include copies of overhead projections in handouts
- The main points written on the board
- New terms and/or vocabulary written on the board
- Writing on boards and/or overhead projections to be large and clear
- New information to be delivered more than once. Over-learning – going over the same material again and again – is often necessary
- Students to be allowed to use tape recorders or laptop computers during lectures
- Helpers or other students to be permitted to take notes on behalf of students with dyspraxia
- Provision of multi-sensory material which can be absorbed more easily than speech or written material alone
- Video tapes to be used, to be borrowed for repeat viewing

- Understanding that noise, movement and visual clutter may distract
- Encouragement to ask questions
- Students with dyspraxia to be allowed longer time to think and frame responses
- Reading priorities to be indicated so that the most important texts get read first.

WRITING ESSAYS AND ASSIGNMENTS

- Help provided with structure and organisation
- Existing essays and reports offered as examples
- Advice given on the most useful books on a reading list, so that the student is not overwhelmed
- Work to the student's strengths in order to build self-esteem
- Spelling mistakes pointed out, but the main focus to be on the content rather than on the presentation. A quiet space such as a cubicle or carrel in the library can also help the student concentrate when there are many distractions around and so produce better work.

PRACTICAL WORK

Many students with dyspraxia have greater difficulty with gross motor skills than with fine motor skills, so are able to cope with tasks that involve manual dexterity. However, the college has a responsibility to ensure that all its students can handle equipment in the kitchen or laboratory safely.

- Equipment could be held onto a firm base with clamps
- Containers and fragile equipment could be stabilised on non-slip plastic mats
- Food processors could be used instead of knives to chop, slice and grate food
- Mastering a sewing machine may take time and patience for tutor and student. Ultimately machine

stitching is often easier than hand sewing for a student with dyspraxia

- Procedures and sequences may need to be demonstrated a number of times

- Students with dyspraxia can find following instructions difficult. Many like to write down the steps to be taken

- The presence of a helper, and/or individual tuition, can be useful.

> *I am very poor at tasks which require manual skills. I was nearly thrown out of my postgraduate town planning course because of my lack of drawing ability.*
>
> Gordon

Make lists of all the things you have to do and hang them on the wall in a prominent place

Organise your studies

A study-skills class is a good way to build confidence and experience with personal organisation in every aspect of academic life. You can also watch what other people do and ask them what works. Students with dyspraxia have recommended these strategies for getting organised:

A study-skills class is a good way to build confidence and experience

- Buy a pack of plastic wallets with holes punched in them and a hardback folder with cardboard dividers. Label each of the dividers. As soon as you get a handout at a lecture, put it in a plastic wallet and file it in the folder. Do not punch holes in the handouts themselves – they will break and get lost. Label each plastic folder with the title of the lecture, or its contents.

- Colour-coding your files might prevent you losing them and their contents – say, red for marketing, blue for history. You could even stick coloured spots on the spines of your textbooks.

- Keep a diary with a page for each day. Note down all the things you have to do. Mark the most important with a colour and do those first. Tick off the things you have done and then reward yourself.

- Make lists of all the things you have to do and hang them on the wall in a prominent place. Post-It notes can be very useful for this.

- You could try using a dictaphone to record messages to yourself.

- Plan ahead your day, week and month.

- Decide what is important. Then go ahead and do it, even if you don't want to – but reward yourself!

- Build in enough time to complete tasks.

- Don't set yourself goals which are too ambitious.

To pick up errors, read your essays aloud slowly

Note-taking

- Do not try and write down every word.

- Try to develop the skill of taking the notes in diagrammatic form using spidergrams or mind maps.

- Get permission to tape the lecture.

- Use a laptop to take notes.

- Ask people who understand your problems to lend you their notes.

If note-taking is really difficult you might consider paying somebody to take notes for you.

Essays and assignments

Study-skills classes are likely to teach you:

- how to analyse, and write to, an essay title

- how to plan an essay

- how to proofread effectively.

To pick up errors, read your essays aloud slowly. Read them several times: once for spelling; once for content; and once for sentence structure.

Mind maps

Essay writing, along with note-taking and revision planning, may become easier if you use mind maps. These incorporate pictures, colour and a few words, and help you to memorise things and use more of your brain power.

You will need a large blank piece of paper and different-coloured pens and pencils. Write or draw the main topic in the centre. Less important details should be put towards the edge of the paper. Doing this enables you to see clearly what needs to be done and the steps to take to achieve the result. Extra information can be added at any time.

Example of a mind map:

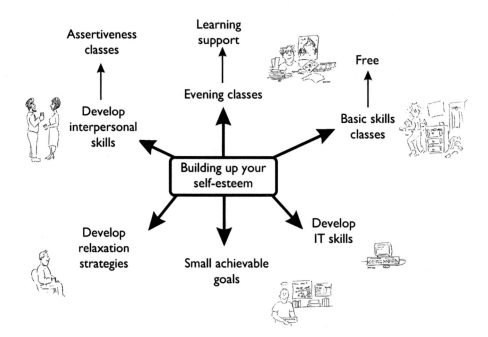

The Speed-Reading Book by Tony Buzan (2003). London: BBC Active.

The Ultimate Book of Mind Maps by Tony Buzan (2002). London: Thorsons.

Planning and Organization – Problems and Solutions by Jan Poustie (1999). Taunton: Next Generation.

Revising for examinations

- Revise with friends and discuss your ideas. Go through question papers together.

- Break down information into manageable chunks.

- Take frequent breaks from revision – every 30 to 40 minutes.

- Mnemonics – stringing together initials and making a word or phrase from them can be very useful memory joggers. If you have a list to remember, imagine and commit to memory a picture from that list. The more ridiculous the image, the easier it will be to remember.

- Use as many of your senses as possible when revising. As well as reading, tape record key notes, and watch (or record for yourself) relevant videos.

- Do as many timed practice exams as you can.

Use Your Memory: Understanding Your Mind to Improve Memory and Mental Power by Tony Buzan (2003). London: BBC Books.

How to Mind Map. The Ultimate Thinking Tool that will Change Your Life by Andrew Wright (2002). London: HarperCollins.

www.brainhe.com. Best Resources for Achievement and Intervention re Neurodiversity in Higher Education. A national resource centre for staff and students with specific learning differences at university.

The internet has opened up tremendous opportunities for students with dyspraxia

Technology can help

The internet has opened up tremendous opportunities for students with dyspraxia to access and retrieve information far more directly than through reading text. Programs for PCs are available to support your learning and acquisition of study skills.

AbilityNet, PO Box 94, Warwick CV34 5WS. Tel: 0800 269 545, www.abilitynet.co.uk. Makes computer technology available to people with disabilities.

Computer Information and Advice Service, 98 London Road, Reading RG1 5AU. Tel: 0118 966 2677

WORD PROCESSORS

Students with poor handwriting can present work neatly using a word processor. Programmes such as Word feature good spell checkers which underline misspelt words. Grammar checkers assume a certain amount of knowledge, but can be useful if you have a tendency to miss out essential words. Laptops can enable you to take notes straight onto the computer (see above).

COMPUTER MICE

Mice come in a variety of shapes and sizes. It is a good idea to try them out before buying one, or choosing the most comfortable and efficient one at college. A cordless mouse is easier to use. An anti-slip mouse mat can help with mouse control. A mouse can be slowed to make it easier to manipulate. If you have a mechanial mouse, ensure that it works properly by cleaning it out regularly, taking out its ball and blowing out the fluff. Some mice that have proved useful for dyspraxic people are the rollerball mouse and the Anir (which acts a bit like a joystick so that you can have more control over it).

Optical mice are very smooth and easy to use: they will work on almost any surface, and do not need cleaning.

Students with poor handwriting can present work neatly using the word processor

KEYBOARDS

People with co-ordination problems often use ergonomic keyboards more easily than standard ones. Key guards can be added to stop you striking the wrong keys. Keyboards with a wrist rest help people with poor muscle tone and can prevent RSI (repetitive strain injury).

There are an enormous number of programs to assist with note-taking and written work

COLOUR OVERLAYS

Colour overlays that fit over the screen can prevent text from appearing blurred or distorted. Find out which colour overlay gives you the greatest benefit.

MONITORS

You can change the background colour and typematter on most computers. Special monitors are available for those who are colour sensitive: ideally they should have at least 17-inch screens to accommodate larger print.

SCANNERS

Flatbed scanners enable students to scan in pages of books and handouts. You can then edit, reorganise and highlight the text. The scanners can complement speech-to-text software such as Kurzweil 3000.

Computer software

There is an enormous number of programs to assist with note-taking and written work. You may need to take some time to become accustomed to using them, particularly the voice-activated programs. People with dyspraxia and dyslexia have found the following selection of programs helpful. All of these are available from iANSYST (Tel: 01223 420101, www.dyslexic.com). This company specialises in software for people with dyslexia and will discuss your personal needs with you. They are also available from Jeff Hughes, Box 42, Special Needs Computing (Tel: 0151 426 9988, www.box42.com). Other suppliers include the Dyscovery Centre Newport (Tel: 01633 432 330, www.dyscoverycentre.co.uk).

PLANNING PROGRAMS

To use planning programs to the full you need to have access to a colour printer.

Mind Genius, Mind Manager and Mindfull help to create and communicate ideas. A powerful diagram view lets you express your ideas visually, whilst simultaneously creating an organised outline. It is a great planning tool for those who think visually.

VOICE-ACTIVATED SOFTWARE

Dragon Dictate Naturally Speaking Professional 8: dictation programs like this require much less training than other dictation programs, which make you pause after each word.

IBM ViaVoice 10 Professional. It enables features of Microsoft Word and other Microsoft programs such as fonts and bullet points to be controlled by verbal command.

PRESENTATION AND WRITING

MS Publisher provides a range of very useful templates for all sorts of written documents, projects and posters.

TEXT TO SPEECH AND PREDICTIVE SOFTWARE

TEXT TO SPEECH AND PREDICTIVE SOFTWARE

Texthelp Read and Write 7.1 gold not only reads text back to you, but also finds spelling mistakes missed by other spell checkers and can predict up to ten words at a time.

Penpal XL will read text back to you and also predicts, which can improve your accuracy and saves time (Microsoft Word also has a tool for word prediction).

Kurzweil 3000 Personal Reader is a reading machine, independent of your computer, which translates typewritten material such as letters, books and newspapers.

STUDYING

Wordswork helps you to acquire study skills.

All of the programs listed above except MSPublisher are available from iANSYST – see above for details.

Touch Type Read and Spell is a systematic programme of seeing, speaking and typing – a computer course for reading and spelling development through touch-typing. Tel: 020 8464 7330, www.ttrs.co.uk.

Stick-IT is an orgamisational and planning software package that can be helpful in organising your revision, study schedules and tasks and is available from the Dyscovery Centre (see above for details.)

Tuition and Training runs typing courses specifically for dyspraxics. Tel: 020 8858 9180.

Useful equipment

Electronic personal organisers can be used as a diary, addresses store and shopping list. You can set alarms to remind you to do particular tasks. The disadvantage of most organisers is their very small keyboards. You might prefer to use the planner facilities in Microsoft Office.

Buy a calculator with a large display area and large buttons. Shops such as WHSmith sell talking calculators, and those with a print-out facility, which are useful if you tend to press the wrong buttons. Voice-activated calculators will be with us soon!

A recorder/mini-disk player that will link up to a computer for transcription of spoken material can be very helpful for lectures or meetings.

Step Pad can be useful as it will record and playback sequences of reminder messages (available from www. Enablemart.com).

Watch Minder 2 is another useful gadget for people with little sense of time – it is a watch which can be timed to go off in a sequence of set times (available from the Dyscovery Centre: see above for details.

Listening Books Library. Tel: 020 7407 9417, www.listening-books.org.uk. For a large selection of books on tape and CD.

Barrybennett.com has a great deal of useful equipment for students such as magnifier reading rulers and ergonomic keyboards.

Mathematics for Dyslexics, A Teaching Handbook by S.J. Chinn and J.R. Ashcroft (1993). London: Whurr.

The Changing Face of Dyslexia in Higher Education: A Digest and Commentary on the Report of the National Working Party on Dyslexia in Higher Education by Debbie Gibberd and Charmaine Michelson (1999). London: City University.

Dyslexia at College by Dorothy Gilroy and Tim Miles (1995). London: Routledge.

> *Dyspraxia is not a disability, it is a learning difficulty. The big danger is that you learn to lean on the support of others and do not develop the drive and determination which are the major compensating characteristics. Coupled with a belief in oneself, which the right sort of guidance can bring about, then the dyspraxic can do very well in life.*
>
> Wendy

Chapter 8

Dyspraxia at Work

Starting with their problems in completing job application forms and with presenting themselves effectively in interviews, dyspraxic people can experience particular difficulties at work. (As we have stressed throughout this book, they also possess a range of skills and strengths.)

These difficulties include:

- organising yourself and your work – the untidiest desk in the office will be yours
- doing practical tasks such as photocopying and using date stamps
- operating computers
- understanding office systems
- following and remembering instructions
- remembering telephone numbers, meetings and appointments
- keeping to schedules and deadlines
- taking messages
- needing to constantly rewrite letters and reports

- losing the thread of discussions in meetings
- relating to colleagues.

In short, we often baffle our employers completely.

Jobs and careers – Getting started
Choosing the right job

Whether you are starting out at work or want to change direction, you probably know what your strengths and talents are and what you enjoy. It may not be easy to see how this knowledge can lead you to the right career or job.

Choosing the right kind of work or career is a big challenge for most people. For those with dyspraxia, conventional career options may not be suitable. You may want to avoid the jobs where there is a lot of pressure to perform or to conform; which require you to work in a busy open-plan office; or which involve good balance or co-ordination.

Make a list of your qualifications, your experience and your strengths and skills

> *I was sacked from a factory because I was too slow and I couldn't work in a shop because I had problems with maths.*
>
> Shirley

If you find a job which really motivates you, with a mission that you truly believe in, you are likely to find that organising yourself in work goes more smoothly.

To assess your abilities, make a list of your qualifications, your experience and your strengths and skills. Show the list to your family and friends – they may tell you still more about your abilities.

List all the experience you have gained through paid jobs and voluntary work. Try to view your experiences and the way you are in a positive light. You may have used a computer from an early age to avoid writing by hand – so you have experience with computers!

Many people with dyspraxia are determined, hard-working and original thinkers. You may have artistic or creative ability, strong visual awareness, or good verbal skills. It may be possible to turn a hobby such as photography or writing into a potential job. You might want to consider work in the caring professions – helping those with disabilities, or working with elderly people or with animals.

In most jobs, social skills are as important as competence. You may need to improve social skills before you apply for your chosen career, to strengthen your chances of success. See Chapter 4 for help with this.

If you left school without qualifications, ask for details of courses at your local college of further education or adult education institute. These colleges may be better equipped to meet your needs than schools were in the past.

You can ask for help filling forms

> *I left college and became an office junior. Everything was mis-filed, and when I filled in people's hours on the timesheets everything went in the wrong column. However (they said) I was the best telephonist they ever had! They ended up keeping me on switchboard duties and assigned what they felt was too 'complicated' to the other young people in the office. I loved phone work but felt belittled because I couldn't do something a simple as keeping time records.*
>
> Karen

Your CV and job applications

You can ask for help with filling in forms from the Careers Service, Connexions or Jobcentre Plus.

You may be able to scan an application form into a computer and fill it in on-screen. If not, photocopy the form several times so that you can make rough copies. You could use one copy to work out how you will space the information, and how many words will fit into each section. Check the copies for the sequence of information, spelling, vocabulary and construction of sentences. On the final version you can just concentrate on making your handwriting neat. It is important that your completed form looks pleasing.

Employers could help applicants with dyspraxia by:

- printing application forms in clear typeface on pastel coloured paper to reduce glare

- sending application forms by disk or e-mail if handwriting legibility is not relevant to the job

- allowing extra time for the candidate in testing

- letting somebody write for them.

Interviews

As well as briefing yourself as much as possible about your potential employer, you can prepare yourself for the interview.

- If the employing organisation is large, ask the human resources department for an equal opportunities statement or ask a Careers Officer to do it for you. Look for references to disability and particularly to specific learning difficulties. Find out from human resources what support and training would be available.

Practise interview techniques through role-playing

- Prepare yourself mentally for the interview. Think very hard about what you believe you could contribute to the job.

- Practise interview techniques through role-playing with a teacher, supportive friend or relation. This will help you to improve eye contact and to present yourself in the best possible light.

- Decide on suitable clothes well before the interview. Brand-new clothes can be stiff and distracting. Ensure that what you wear is comfortable, clean and well pressed. Avoid shoes which have a high narrow heel or a large platform sole, as you may trip in them.

- Work out in detail how you will get to the interview. Allow plenty of time for the journey, and make sure you have the right money for the fare.

Help with choosing a career

CAREERS SERVICES/CONNEXIONS

Careers Services are independent companies that receive funding from the government and must meet national standards. You will find Careers Services under 'Careers' in your phone book. For under-19s go to 'Connexions' (www.connexions.gov.uk).

Careers Services deal with adults as well as school leavers; and most have a Special Needs Careers Adviser who has experience of advising people with disabilities and who can give you general information about different types of jobs and how to apply for them. If you are at college, the careers advice service will be able to help you.

Careers Services deal with adults with special needs, Connexions deals with 13- to 19-year-olds

You could also ask your local Citizens Advice Bureau about local organisations that may be able to help you, and about support organisations which provide coaches and/or support workers when you start a job or do work experience. Job coaches make sure that instructions are given clearly and can give you extra training if you need it. They can also advise you on building up good relations with your work colleagues and on coping effectively with work-related anxieties.

EMPLOYMENT SERVICE – NOW JOBCENTRE PLUS

Most Jobcentres have a Disability Service Team (DST), now called Disability Services and Financial Team, which includes an occupational psychologist and a Disability Employment Adviser (DEA). The role of the DST is to provide advice and assistance to people with disabilities who want to work or to get experience of working. The DSTs work with people with a wide range of disabilities, so some will be better informed than others about dyspraxia.

The DEA is a good starting-point. When you visit the DEA, take along your CV or make some notes about your qualifications and the dates you started and finished jobs. Your notes should also include:

- a list of your strengths
- ideas about the support you think you may need

- a leaflet about dyspraxia

- a friend or relative to support you.

Funds to help dyspraxic employees are available through the Access to Work scheme, to cover training costs and purchase of equipment. To make an application, contact the Access to Work Business Centre. (Funds are also available for self-employed people.)

Before you offer the leaflet to the DEA, ask whether they would like information about dyspraxia. If you just hand over the leaflet they might think that you are questioning their ability to do their job.

You need to emphasise how your dyspraxia conceals your real strengths and intelligence. It is very easy for people to assume that you are less intelligent than you really are especially if you are reticent and find that expressing yourself is difficult. The DEA may pass you on to the occupational psychologist for assessment of your abilities.

It is very easy to assume that you are less intelligent than you really are

DEAs can advise you about the training courses run by the learning and Skills Council in England and by the Scottish Executive and Welsh Assembly in their respective countries. The courses can help you to train in a particular skill and lead on to qualifications such as NVQS or GNVQs. Some of the courses are run at residential training colleges.

DEAs may discuss with you whether you are eligible to take part in the New Deal projects that have been introduced for people who have been on Jobseeker's Allowance for at least six months and/or a sickness-related benefit. (Participants in the New Deal have their own adviser for the duration of their involvement.)

Under the Supported Employment Scheme part of my wages are paid by the Employment Service. This means that I was employed by people who normally wouldn't have considered me, because of my slowness and difficultly with communication.

Philip

They may also advise you about whether you are eligible to take part in Access to Work and on self-employment options.

You may be eligible for supported employment (now called Workstep) if your dyspraxia is severe and you find it difficult to keep a job in the open market. Again, the DEA will guide you through this and various other options. They can also advise you about the practicalities of self-employment – an option which many people with dyspraxia find suits them well if they have help with administration.

Supported employment offers the opportunity of working in many different types of jobs at your own pace, in the way that suits you best. Fields where supported employment is available include horticulture, catering and office work. Employment is usually by a local authority or voluntary organisation that has a contract with the Jobcentre Plus which sponsors you in your work and provides training. You will be paid the same wages as other employees who do similar work.

Your DEA can arrange for you to be assessed for a suitable job by an occupational psychologist

Access to Work Business Centre. Tel: 020 8218 2710.

Employment Service Direct. Tel: 0845 606 0234, www.employmentservice.gov.uk. A service for people who are not in work.

New Deal for Disabled People. Tel: 0845 606 2626, www.newdeal.gov.uk/nddp.

Residential Training Unit. Tel: 0191 202 3579. For details of residential training courses.

Your DEA can also arrange for you to be assessed for a suitable job by an occupational psychologist: see Chapter 2 for details of what this assessment would entail. Alternatively, a private assessment from an occupational psychologist would show in detail where your strengths and weaknesses lie, and point you towards suitable occupations.

Organisations that help disabled job seekers include:

Association of Disabled Professionals. Tel: 01204 431638, www.adp.org.uk. Helps disabled people to find and retain work.

Basic Skills Agency. Tel: 020 7405 4017, www.basic-skills.co.uk. Encourages the running of courses on reading, writing and maths to the level necessary for progress at work.

British Association for Supported Employment. www.afse.org.uk.

Connexions. Tel: 0808 001 3219, www.connexions.gov.uk. A new service for young people (13–19) in England, giving advice on careers and general welfare. It is administered through local partnerships and brings together the work of many government agencies and voluntary organisations. For more information, try your local careers office or youth services.

Coverdale Organization plc. Tel: 0800 298 9778, www.coverdale.co.uk. Runs the leadership development programme for disabled people who want to develop their teamwork and management skills.

Disabled Entrepreneurs. www.disabled-enrepreneurs.net. Aims to provide networking opportunities for self-employed disabled people.

Employers' Forum on Disability. Tel: 020 7403 3020, www.employers-forum.co.uk. Produces a practical guide to employment adjustments for people with dyslexia, useful for dyspraxics too.

Employment Opportunities. www.opportunities.org.uk. An employment service for disabled graduates.

Jobcentre Plus. Tel: 0845 606 0234 (helpline), www.jobcentreplus.gov.uk.

LearnDirect. Tel: 0800 100 900, www.learnindirect.co.uk. offers individual careers advice and free courses on computers.

Mencap, national centre. Tel: 020 7454 0454, www.mencap.org.uk. Some areas have Mencap Pathway employment advisers.

Prince's Trust. Tel: 0800 842 842, www.princes-trust.org.uk. Gives grants and support for people under 30 setting up their own business.

RADAR. Tel: 020 7250 3222, www.radar.org.uk. Publishes information on services for disabled people including employment.

Remploy Ltd. Tel: 0800 138 7656, www.remploy.co.uk. Supported employment through Workstep scheme.

Shaw Trust. Tel: 01225 716350, www.shaw-trust.org.uk. Training, work experience and placements to disabled people and to people who have had mental health problems.

Skill. Tel: 0800 328 5050, www.skill.org.uk. Information on training and work for students with disabilities. Publishes excellent information leaflets.

Workable. Tel: 020 7553 0002, www.workable.co.uk. Graduate support scheme for the disabled.

To disclose, or not to disclose?

DANDA is often asked whether or not dyspraxia should be disclosed to employers. This is never an easy question to answer as each person's circumstances are unique.

These pros and cons could help you to decide about disclosure, if you are not applying for sheltered or similar work. You could discuss with your DEA or Careers Adviser whether or not to disclose your dyspraxia.

If you decide to disclose, do so in a positive way

If you decide to disclose, do so in a positive way, putting across your eligibility for the job.

REASONS TO DISCLOSE

- Many job application forms and medical questionnaires ask direct questions about disability and health. If you give false information and your employer finds out, you may risk dismissal, especially if your dyspraxia is of a moderate or severe nature.

- Many employers have an equal opportunities policy which shows that they are committed to recruiting and employing people without prejudice. Some employers are keen to employ disabled people. If the job involves working with disabled people, your disability could be an asset. Look out for the two-ticks disability symbol in job adverts. The Employers' Forum on Disability (see above) has a list of these 'positive' employers.

- Telling the interviewers about your dyspraxia could work in your favour, as they may then adapt your interview to give you a better chance. For example, they may ignore any problems that you have in maintaining eye contact.

- Disclosure may help to ensure that your performances at interview, and in work, are more fairly assessed. You will probably find the work less stressful as a result.

- Employers are required to make reasonable adaptations to accommodate your disability. These adaptations may well enable you to do your job better. Accommodations cannot be made if you do not disclose.

- Early disclosure can save you embarrassment, and give your manager and colleagues the opportunity to be understanding and tolerant. They will need to know that procedures should be explained to you clearly and logically, and given to you in writing if possible.

REASONS NOT TO DISCLOSE

- You may feel that your disability will have no effect on your ability to do the job, and that you will not need your employer to make adaptations for you.

- If competition for the job is fierce, you may decide that disclosure would put you at a disadvantage.

- You may believe the prospective employer has pre-set ideas about disability, or would regard you as a liability and a possible source of expense. Some employers look no further than a person's disabilities and fail to see their abilities.

Coming out of the closet was hard and the decision took a long time; now I'm glad. I know where I stand with people. At first I got some strange reactions. Either people were very supportive or they ran a mile, not sure how to react. I guess it could be put down to the lack of understanding. I found being honest was the best policy.

Clare

Disability Discrimination Act

The Disability Discrimination Act defines a person with a disability as having 'a physical or mental impairment which has substantial and long-term adverse effect on his [sic] ability to carry out normal day-to-day activities'. The abilities which are mentioned as affecting day-to-day activities include manual dexterity, and impairments of mind, memory or ability to concentrate.

We have received written confirmation from the Prime Minister's Office that if a person with dyspraxia complies with the above definition of a disabled person, they are covered by the Act. The government recognises dyspraxia as a valid medical disorder, as defined by the World Health Organization's International Classification of Disease.

The government recognises dyspraxia as a valid medical disorder

The Act also states that all reasonable adjustments should be made to accommodate disabled people. Reasonable adjustments could include:

- altering working hours to times when there are fewer distractions

- acquiring and modifying equipment such as computers to include speech input

- providing a support worker to help those who lack confidence

- allowing absences during work to receive treatment

- giving or arranging training

- transferring the person to fill a vacancy to which they are more suited

- modifying instructions and the ways they are given.

The employer will take into account the cost of making the adjustments and of the practical use they will be for the person concerned.

The Act applies to all employment matters, including recruitment, training, promotion and dismissal. Those who feel they have been discriminated against can complain to an industrial tribunal within three months of the discriminatory act. In 2005, the Disability Discrimination Act 2005 amended the DDA 1995 to place a duty on all public bodies to promote equality of opportunity for disabled people. The Disability Equality Duty (as it is known) will come into force on 5 December 2006 and should have a beneficial effect on how disabled people are treated – at least in the public sector.

In April 2000 the government set up the Disability Rights Commission (DRC) whose main function is the elimination of discrimination against disabled people. The Human Rights Act, which came into force in October 2000, further strengthened the rights of those who have a disability. In 2005, the DRC set up a neuro-diversity/autistic spectrum disorder action group which includes dyspraxia.

i   Advisory, Conciliation and Arbitration Services (ACAS). Tel: 08457 47 47 47, www.acas.org.uk.

Disability Rights Commission. Tel: 0845 762 2633, www.drc-gb.org.

Trade unions

Many trade unions have policies which support those with disabilities. Some unions have a list of coping strategies which were devised for people with dyslexia and will be useful for those with dyspraxia. Your union representative, if you have one, should be able to tell you about this.

If your union has no policy in place, you could:

- ask whether a combined policy on dyslexia and dyspraxia can be drafted with your help, to be raised at the next branch meeting and put forward at the next AGM

- find out if your representative has received any specific training in representing people with disabilities

- put your own name forward to go on a training course to help people with disabilities. The TUC's National Education Centre provides such a course

- ask to obtain the training materials used by unions such as USDAW for people with dyslexia which will benefit those with dyspraxia too.

Many trade unions have policies which support those with disabilities

i Trades Union Congress. Tel: 020 7636 4030, www.tuc.org.uk.

USDAW (Union of Shop, Distributive and Allied Workers). Tel: 0161 224 2804/249 2400, www.usdaw.org.uk.

How to cope in the workplace

If your dyspraxia is mild, you may find that you just work in a different way to your colleagues. People with more severe dyspraxia will find the support of a sympathetic employer and/or manager is invaluable.

Employees with dyspraxia are often determined, persistent and highly motivated, and may be creative and original. Their approach to problems tends to be holistic, rather than following through sequences and getting bogged down in detail.

Relaxation techniques can help you to be calm and positive

Relaxation techniques can help you to approach your tasks and your colleagues in a calm and positive manner, and to improve your efficiency. See Chapter 3 for ideas on relaxation.

How to follow instructions and learn new procedures

- Ask for practical projects to be demonstrated. Expect to be supervised for these kinds of projects.

- When using new equipment – telephone system, fax machine, photocopier – make a list or chart of the procedures. Stick them up by the machine or keep the directions in a drawer, to save you the embarrassment of asking colleagues repeatedly how to operate it. You may end up helping other people!

- Ask for a series of instructions to be given to you one at a time.

- Repeat back the instructions to the person who gave them to you.

- Use mnemonics to help you to remember sequences.

- Write down the instruction (clearly, with spaces, bullet points, headings, highlights, etc., or in a flow-chart format).

- Ask for summaries and key points rather than full reports, to circumvent short-term memory problems.

- Take notes of instructions and then get them checked.

- Training and new methods of working can be presented visually as flow-charts or diagrams, or through a video.

> *Guess who stuck labels on the photocopier trays! I wasn't the only one who could never remember the right way up to put the headed paper.*
>
> Jessica

How to get organised and improve time-keeping

- Ask for training in time management and in strategies to compensate for poor memory. You could find out about courses on these yourself and present them to your line manager.

- Decide how long a task should take.

- Use a timer (on your computer?) to keep to deadlines.

- Build planning time into each day.

- Have a 'to do' list.

- Break down a big job into smaller sections and give yourself frequent rests.

- Give yourself a reward when you have finished a difficult task.

- Ask for extra time to operate machines and equipment, and to complete tasks.

- Multi-sensory equipment, such as a talking calculator, can be helpful.

- In the office, make sure you have plenty of shelves and storage space.

- Hang a wall planner that highlights visually your day-to-day and regular appointments, your projects and deadlines.

- Colour-code your files and their contents.

- Encourage the adoption of a 'buddy' system whereby colleagues help each other.

Give yourself a reward when you have finished a difficult task

> *Some colleagues have adapted unconsciously to my ways. One was looking for a file. 'It's on the right-hand side of my desk,' I said confidently. She went automatically to the left-hand side to find it.*
>
> Jenny

Communication

Every organisation has its own unwritten rules and procedures. There are those who really have the power, and there are those who are only nominally in charge. Try to make sure that you do not end up on the wrong side of your office's inner circle.

Make sure that you do not end up on the wrong side of your office's inner circle

It is not easy for many adult dyspraxics to interpret subtle nuances of practice and behaviour. You may need to ask for help from someone more experienced in these than yourself. Identifying key people, understanding the politics, and approaching those people in the right way are especially important if you want to bring about change in the workplace, and to achieve what you want without upsetting them. Some dyspraxics can be impulsive, too ready to challenge authority and to question policies or procedures.

Go for training in communication skills or assertiveness, or both. Training can help dyspraxics who are aggressive to curb their impulsiveness, as well as support those who are passive.

Writing reports and letters

In addition to training in practical and personal skills, tuition may be available in improving report writing, spelling and grammar. If possible, get a colleague to proofread your work and to help you to spot errors.

Technology is terrific

Computers can be an invaluable tool. As well as spelling and grammar checkers, you can set up templates for your letters and other documents and projects and use the diary features to remind and prioritise. Find out from the computer specialist what features can make your working life easier. If your handwriting is difficult to read, ask if you can use a word processor instead of a pen. See Chapter 7 for more details.

Get rid of distractions

Try to make sure that your workstation is situated away from loud machinery, busy telephones and other distractions. You could ask if you can go somewhere quiet, such as a library or a store room to finish a project. Ask your manager to encourage co-workers not to disturb you.

If you still find that working is difficult amidst the day-to-day noise and distractions, ask if you could come in earlier or stay later, so that you can work when it is quieter, or whether you could work from home. If you need to concentrate particularly hard in the office, you could use earphones or you could ask for a screen to be put around your desk.

If you experience difficulties at work because of your dyspraxia, your employer may want to assess your strengths and weaknesses at work. The Disability Services Team (DST) from your local Jobcentre may be able to assess you, and recommend any changes that will help you in your work environment. Your employer may bring in an occupational psychologist for the assessment.

Employers can apply for funding from the Access to Work scheme for adapting equipment for use by people with disabilities.

Able to Succeed: Disabilities, Health and Job Choice by Sarah Bosley (2004). Loughborough: CASCAiD. Mainly for careers officers but useful for people with disabilities too.

The Adult Dyslexic: Interventions and Outcomes by David McLoughlin, Carol Leather and Patricia Stringer (2002). Chichester: Wiley.

Asperger Syndrome Employment Workbook: An Employment Workbook for Adults with Asperger Syndrome by Roger N. Meyer (2000). London: Jessica Kingsley Publishers.

BDA Employer's Guide to Dyslexia 2005. Order from www.r-e-m.co.uk/bda.

Dyslexia in the Workplace by Diana Bartlett and Sylvia Moody (2000). Chichester: Wiley. Includes a chapter on dyspraxia.

Dyslexia in the Workplace – A Guide for Unions by Brian Hagan (2005). London: TUC Briefing. Includes a section on dyspraxia.

Moving into Work (2006). Disability Alliance. A guide covering support available for disabled people wanting to move into work and self-employment. Tel: 020 7247 9776, www.disabilityalliance.org.

The Hidden Disabilities Toolkit - Resource Pack. This covers dyspraxia and related conditions in the workplace and discusses coping strategies and adjustments to improve performance. Key4learning (2003). Tel 01285 720 964, www.key4learning.com.

Transition: Employment and Job Retention for Young People with Developmental Co-ordination Disorder/Dyspraxia and Related Conditions published by the Dyscovery Centre, 2001.

i Skill. Tel: 0800 328 5050, www.skill.org.uk. Publishes many booklets and leaflets about disabled people and work.

Chapter 9

FOUR ADULTS WITH DYSPRAXIA

The stories and the comments scattered through this book are drawn from the experiences of many dyspraxic people. In this chapter, adults with dyspraxia speak for themselves at greater length. They show how negative experience can be overcome and how, in coming to an understanding of dyspraxia, people can step out into the light and lead positive and achieving lives.

Jean

Does anyone have any answers?

How do you begin to express the pain and frustration of a lifetime striving and struggling to achieve an impossibility: to carry out what are normal, everyday tasks to the majority of people on this planet?

How do you begin to explain to people what hinders and frustrates you, when you have had no one to sit down with you and explain that something is malfunctioning some-where?

No one can tell me why I am how I am. I have had no professional help. My doctor doesn't understand my difficulty. I don't know whether anyone ever will.

These words are written by Jean, who eloquently expresses the questions and the difficulties that must haunt all of us who live with dyspraxia. We know that something hinders us and often we believe that that something is our fault. The resulting bewilderment can be maddening: it is as if a cancer eats away at our self-esteem. We want to know why our problems exist, but there seem to be no answers out there.

Jean continues:

> I came up against difficulties when I tried to learn how to drive: I still can't do it after years of trying. Career choice has been limited. At the threshold of adulthood I couldn't achieve my dreams and goals because of difficulties with the areas that I couldn't make function.

> I had problems with perception, judging depth and distance, balance, poor reflexes. I had learning difficulties with maths and counting money; verbal communication difficulties; and low self-esteem. My brain seemed not to function at times – it felt as if I was hitting my head against a wall.

> Even today, as an adult, I find everyday tasks frustrating and difficult, even impossible. For some things, I have been able to find tools or strategies for coping. But in other areas I still can't achieve, and some I avoid altogether.

> I still have problems with attempting driving, learning the computer, typing, using keys, opening cans, peeling vegetables, doing buttons and zips, changing light bulbs, tying knots and shoelaces, measuring things, and judging distances or depths. I also find it difficult to express myself.

> I am capable, intelligent, gifted and perceptive in other areas, yet I am branded stupid, clumsy and slow by relatives, teachers and peers and by people who don't know me and who see me struggle to do things. I get very down and there are days that I despair at myself.

> There is no one who really understands how it is for me. My friends try to understand and support me but on bad days even they can't help.

> Is there anyone out there who can explain to me why no one in the medical field believes me? Surely in these enlightened years someone can give me an answer.

Since she wrote this, there have been developments in Jean's life.

My life has taken on new direction thanks to you all at the Adult Support Group. I was eventually able to get my GP to listen and to refer me to a consultant neurologist, who immediately arranged for his senior occupational therapist to take me under her wing. I'm now in ongoing occupational therapy which I find really helpful. I also hope to take a voice-activated computer course, and my DEA is trying to arrange funding for this.

Martin

Martin is 45 years old. His dyspraxia was diagnosed privately in 1995.

Martin had originally been tested for dyslexia. He says the reason was 'my inability to find employment and to acquire the skills to do certain types of jobs. I had counselling for mild depression, and I decided that I might be dyslexic.'

After leaving school Martin had attended a polytechnic where he gained a 2:1 degree in Humanities.

> As a student I joined the Anarchist Society and was involved in drug taking. Looking back I see that both of these activities were to do with trying to create an identity for myself. The education system I had been through did not give me the skills to cope with the world I found myself in. It left me with the general underlying feeling that I was a failure, and with no idea about how to get a job.

Martin spent 11 years working as a postman in a sorting office.

> I had found the initial training to sort letters very difficult, whilst everybody else had flown through it. I nearly got sacked because of my inability to sort letters to the required standard. Later I had to learn touch typing as part of the Code Sort training. Again, whilst most people had few difficulties, I struggled. This time I failed the course.

Martin left the Post Office and returned to the education system to take an MSc in Computer Science.

> I floundered because of my lack of understanding of maths and inability to think through technical and logical problems. I failed the exams and had to go back and resit them. I gained the Postgraduate Diploma in Information Technology but I did not attempt to do the research to gain the MSc.

He had a period of unemployment and took advantage of government funding to do NVQs in Business Administration, and to do RSA 1 Typing and RSA 1 Word Processing as a way of getting a job in administration.

> Once more I noticed that most people when learning to touch type seem to reach a point where it comes naturally, but this did not happen with me. I also had terrible problems with proofreading, my spelling was not very good, and I made frequent errors which the spell checker did not highlight. Despite all this, I managed to gain the typing qualifications and NVQs then went on to pass Word Processing Level 2. I subsequently attempted RSA 3 but eventually realised that I was never going to reach the required speed of 60–70 words per minute.

> In the meantime, I worked in various temporary secretarial and clerical posts whilst seeking full-time employment. These jobs highlighted my areas of weakness in filing, typing speed, proofreading, and maintaining a consistent approach, as well as undermining my self-confidence.

At the time of writing Martin is working as a Home Carer for social services.

> Even this job is affected by my dyspraxia. When I am cleaning for a partially sighted person I find it difficult to put things back in the same place. I also have to be very careful when collecting pensions and shopping.

> On a happier note I have a successful marriage and a wife who is very supportive, and a stepson who has left home and is married with a successful career.

Martin has come to believe that although his dyspraxia is only mild it has still had a major effect on his life. His coping strategies are:

> Regular exercise, which is useful in developing co-ordination and reducing stress. I am a member of a health club where I use the gym and swimming pool. I find this very beneficial.

> My other strategy is to constantly try new ideas in the job market. It is important to keep at it until you find something you can do without too much trouble. You need to accept your limitations: don't go for promotion unless you are sure you can do the job.

Judith

Judith is in her early thirties. Her problems became apparent when she left school and entered the world of employment.

> I went to London to be a mother's help, and the lady I worked for was very kind and patient with me. After a year doing this I got a job at the Body Shop at Heathrow Airport. I had a very bad time working there because I kept breaking the bottles. In the end it was decided by both parties that I was not suited to this job. What makes me sad is the fact that I tried to tell my employers that I had a problem but they were not interested. Because of this I fell into deep depression and my self-esteem fell to an all time low.

> A few weeks later I started work as a receptionist and I again told them of my difficulties. They were willing to help me up to a point, but they soon lost patience with me and that job was terminated.

At around the same time Judith went to the National Hospital for Neurology and Neurosurgery, London, for a dyslexia test.

> The test lasted about half an hour and the lady said that I could not possibly have dyslexia because I achieved seven O-levels. I protested and said that I had problems with everyday life but she did not want to know. I felt so humiliated, but I was determined to carry on with reception work.

Judith then worked for a year as a receptionist at a college near her home.

> When I passed my driving test – on my sixth attempt! – I decided to get a job working as a nanny. I loved this job and was sad when the family moved away. But I carried on working alone as a childminder until I had my first child.

Judith's daughter was ill when she was born. Despite an operation, the baby died at four days old.

> This compounded my feelings of inadequacy: I felt that I could not even make a baby properly. However, I persevered and eleven months later I had a healthy baby boy.

Judith suffered from severe post-natal depression, and went to see a psychiatrist who arranged for her to have psychotherapy.

> On one visit I explained to her that I wished to find the missing pieces of my jigsaw and find out about my problems. She put me in touch with a psychologist. When I

first met him I still thought we were looking at dyslexia. Then I read a newspaper article about clumsy children. I sent off for the Dyspraxia Foundation's information and I read about ME!

Judith went back to the psychologist and with her new-found information. In June 1994 she received a diagnosis of dyspraxia. She wrote at that time:

I am so thrilled. I am like a new person and I feel totally vindicated. I feel that I can now put those lost years behind me and start afresh. I feel that I owe a huge debt to my daughter because if she had not died I would have never received the help I so desperately needed. I feel she died so that I could lead a better life.

Judith continues:

I was referred to an occupational therapist to investigate my disabilities and to practise skills designed to overcome them. I've discovered I've got a tactile sensory deficiency. This means I can't tell exactly where someone touched me – I'm always a few centimetres out.

I've also got problems with my nerve endings in my fingers. It blocks messages being carried from my brain, causing numbness and explaining why I drop things. I've learned to manage that by improving my grip. Also anything needing simultaneous eye and hand co-ordination causes me problems.

During the eight months I spent with the occupational therapist I was taught cookery, woodwork and craftwork to improve my co-ordination. I can now bake great cakes! I used to turn out cakes that looked like pancakes.

Judith went on to learn the Alexander Technique, which she found helpful, particularly as it slows the body down to make tasks more manageable. She got a job as a learning support assistant in a primary school, helping children with co-ordination problems to work on their motor skills. She finds the children easy to relate to, because they have similar problems to herself.

She wants to emphasise that the improvements in her life are due to a combination of factors: occupational therapy, psychotherapy, the Alexander Technique, non-competitive keeping fit, anti-depressants, and herbal supplements such as Efalex and ginseng.

Janet

Janet Taylor is the unpaid co-ordinator of Dyspraxia Adult's Action in Manchester. She is in her 40s and was diagnosed as dyspraxic in 2000. She was misunderstood as a child: 'I was told that I was an intelligent child but an under-achiever. My parents and teachers thought I was careless and lazy and I did not receive any specialist support.'

Janet's father was a GP and never really understood her difficulties.

> My family were in denial about my dyslexia and dyspraxia. I made a clumsy attempt at learning to dive, while we were on holiday; when dad watched my fairy, elephant belly flops he looked the way he does when observing a patient. He never did anything about my obviously poor co-ordination maybe because he thought I would grow out of it! He said I had a gross inferiority complex with an inadequate personality, without exploring why I felt so hopeless.

Janet had severe difficulties with physical activities as a child: 'I found competitive sports and PE a nightmare and I was always the last to be chosen for the rounders or netball team. I did not learn to ride a bicycle until I was nine or tie my shoelaces until I was twelve.'

She found she was judged at school for her neatness rather than her creativity: 'I found it very frustrating that marks were given for copying the teachers' work neatly off the blackboard and not for original thought'.

Janet underachieved at school and her academic strengths went unrecognised. She was given advice totally inappropriate for a dyspraxic person.

> My career advisor recommended that because I was 'non-academic', I should go into catering which proved to be totally unsuitable. I would have been better doing O-levels and having dyslexia support at my local sixth-form college, but there was no such service.

Janet then took a bakery course, which she just managed to scrape through on the practical side. (The theoretical side was fine.) She saw an advert for catering work in Llandudno and was accepted as a chef. She had a series of jobs in catering and as a chambermaid but was considered too slow and inefficient to keep any for more than a few weeks. The parting words of many employers were: 'Janet, you are a nice girl but you're just not suitable.'

Janet decided to go back to Manchester to look for a community care job.

> Yet again I found the theory easier than the practical and found working with highly physically dependent people a struggle because I had difficulties with dressing, feeding and lifting.

> I decided that working with more physically able people was more suitable for me so I got a job on an unemployment work scheme as a support worker in the special needs department of a community college. I was really good at this – so I did a teaching course for adults with learning difficulties and passed both practical and theory with flying colours, although my written presentation was often criticised for not reflecting my academic ability.

After this work scheme, Janet wanted to continue with the same type of work. However, against her better judgement, she took a job as a residential social worker in a special care unit for people with severe physical and learning difficulties, which meant she had to carry out many practical tasks. She was back in the type of work that exposed her difficulties, and she faced resentment from some members of staff. The stress caused her to become increasingly depressed and she went to see her GP.

> When I told my GP I was uncoordinated and this was causing problems at work, he told me not to worry – it couldn't be that bad because he could read my handwriting. I cheekily asked him if he had co-ordination problems because I couldn't read his!

She then saw a psychiatrist who was dismissive about her co-ordination problems. Janet felt that it was a common misconception among medical professionals to assume that if someone was intelligent, they couldn't have a disability.

Next, she saw a neurologist, through Occupational Health, who diagnosed dyspraxia. The neurologist told her she was 'put together on a Friday night'!

'The neurologist told my employers that I could do the job but there was no mention of dyspraxia. I managed my job with a struggle. Most of my colleagues were friendly but I received constant harassment from a few of them, as they did not understand my disability.' Janet could not explain what her needs were, because she, herself, didn't understand what dyspraxia was, at that point.

Janet continued in this job for seven years, in spite of her low self-esteem, and in spite of being bullied by her colleagues. She became intensely stressed with the intimidating treatment until she was almost incapable of doing the practical part of her job.

Janet was redeployed into a noisy open-plan office where she had difficulty delivering faxes to correct rooms or putting people through to the right extension. She was moved to the accounts office where she had to copy invoice numbers. This lasted two days! Her employers could not find a suitable job for her, so she was medically retired.

> I was so outraged about the way I had been treated that I went to the Internet and found out about Dyspraxia helpline. I phoned Mary Colley, and for the first time I realised that having poor co-ordination was not the only aspect of being dyspraxic, and my other problems were not due to me being careless, lazy and stupid, but were part of my neurological condition.
>
> As a woman living with dyspraxia, I have been unable to learn to drive. I have a poor sense of direction and can't tell right from left. I bump into furniture, get bruises on my legs – and due to short-term memory problems I don't remember getting them. I am sometimes tactless and unintentionally offend people.

However, Janet is a very independent person, and her dyspraxia has not stopped her getting on with her life.

> I own my own house. I do not use my dyspraxia to be the 'helpless female'. I am quite creative visually and have instant sense of colour and design. I do my own decorating and I am quite creative with paint effects and stencils. I have also taught myself to use a computer and the internet and have designed my own website – on adult dyspraxia. I can cook when I concentrate on the task in hand, and I also take part in adventure activities such as white water rafting, abseiling and fire eating!

Janet went on to do a diploma in Community and Youth Work Studies at Manchester University where she was told she was a star pupil – in contrast to the negative labelling she had received before.

I am now a student on the pilot project 'Designing Futures' to help disabled graduates get back into work. The project has also helped me set up my own business, 'Dyspraxia Inclusive Training', to raise awareness of dyspraxia and related conditions and teach personal development to people with neurodiversity.

Janet has now come to terms with her learning differences and feels far more confident. 'Instead of being ashamed of being dyspraxic and hiding that I am different from other people, my life has been transformed from feeling absolutely worthless to being confident enough to teach MSc students and make a living out of becoming a dyspraxia awareness consultant.'

Appendix I

CLAIMING BENEFITS

The benefits most commonly claimed by people with dyspraxia are Disability Living Allowance or Disability Working Allowance, and Incapacity Benefit. You may also be able to claim free travel on public transport.

To be eligible for these benefits your dyspraxia would usually have to be moderate to severe.

Your local Citizens Advice Bureau and/or welfare rights or advocacy service can help you, and make all the difference between success and failure to obtain benefits.

Disability Living Allowance

Applications for Disability Living Allowance (DLA) should be supported by a letter from your GP. It is a non-means-tested benefit. If you are working you can get the Disability Working Allowance. It can be awarded for a fixed term or for life. Anybody under 65 may be entitled to claim it. It is also unaffected by other benefits. There are two components to this benefit: the mobility, and the care. It is the care component of this benefit to which dyspraxia-affected adults would be most likely be entitled, at the lowest rate. The care component is based on the ability to cook a main meal. It is therefore a good idea to spell out the tasks you have difficulty with, in a letter. You could set out an example of a main meal and explain that you have difficulty with tasks such as peeling potatoes, boiling water, lifting hot saucepans, and cutting up vegetables and meat. The likelihood of burning the meal or of scalding yourself should also be mentioned.

The mobility component would be more difficult to get, as it depends on experiencing severe difficulty in walking 200–300 yards. However, if you fall over frequently or need a constant companion because you cannot judge distances when crossing a road or get lost easily, you may be entitled to this component.

If you are turned down for your DLA, it is worth persevering and appealing against the decision. It can take up to 18 months to get to a tribunal. If your DLA is awarded then, the award will be backdated from the date that you first applied. At least half of the appeals for DLA are successful: one person with dyspraxia kept applying and was awarded DLA at the sixth attempt.

Incapacity Benefit

This benefit was introduced in 1995 for people under pensionable age who are unable to work because of illness or disability. To obtain this benefit you will undergo various tests, questionnaires and interviews. In April 2000 the 'personal capability assessment' was introduced, and shifted the emphasis to what you can do rather than what you cannot do. There is also a compulsory work-focused interview for all new benefit claimants.

The rates of Incapacity Benefit vary, from the short-term lower rate through the short-term higher rate, to the long-term rate. People with dyspraxia are unlikely to get the higher rate. Incapacity Benefit is currently being reviewed.

As with Disability Living Allowance, it is worth getting expert advice. If your claim is refused, you have three months to appeal against the decision. In the meantime you may be able to claim Jobseeker's Allowance and Income Support. The system is very complicated and the rules change frequently.

Travel passes

People with dyspraxia can often get reductions on travel on buses and trains. If you live in London, however, you can often get a Freedom Pass which gives you the freedom to travel on the tube, trains and buses over the whole of Greater London. This is easier to obtain if you cannot drive because of your dyspraxia.

For up-to-date details of benefits, get in touch with:

Benefits Enquiry Line. Tel: 0800 88 22 00. For people with disabilities, free and confidential service operated by the Benefits Agency.

Child Poverty Action Group. Tel: 020 7837 7979, www.cpag.org.uk. Publishes the *Welfare Benefits Handbook*.

Citizens Advice Bureau – see your local telephone directory for details.

DIAL UK. Tel: 01302 310123, www.dialuk.org.uk. UK-wide disability information and advice services.

Disability Alliance. Tel: 020 7247 8776, www.disabilityalliance.org.

Disability Law Service. Tel: 020 7791 9800, www.dls.org.uk. Advises on education, benefits, employment and community care.

Disability Living Allowance Helpline. Tel: 08457 123456.

Skill. Tel: 0800 328 5050, www.skill-org.uk.

UK Advocacy Network (UKAN). Tel: 0114 272 8171, www.u-kan.co.uk. Can put you in touch with your local advocacy service.

INDEPENDENT LIVING AND COMMUNITY CARE

Deciding when to leave home can be a very big decision for those with dyspraxia. Parents worry about letting go, and about how their son or daughter will cope when they themselves are too elderly to care for them.

Everybody has a right to develop his or her natural potential and to follow an ordinary pattern of life in the community. You also have the right to be assessed by social services for care in the community. Social services can be your gateway to independent housing. Carers also have a right to be assessed to receive extra help.

Whatever you do, register with your local authority for housing. There are many possibilities: hostels, sheltered housing, respite care, home ownership with support, parental home with support, or residential colleges. Many are run by voluntary organisations.

It is very easy to feel intimidated when you go for a care assessment. Find out as much as you can about the assessment process before your appointment so that you will feel more confident.

Ask for a copy of the criteria that are going to be used for the assessment. You will have the right to talk for as long as you wish, so write down everything that you want to say while you are there. You have to be very clear about what your needs are, and communicate them effectively.

You can ask as many questions as you like, and can take notes. A friend or relative can accompany you.

Ask to receive a copy of the assessment, as you have a right to do so. If you are not satisfied with the outcome, you have a right to complain under the NHS and Community Care Act. Social services and health authorities have separate complaints procedures. Enlist the help of your local Citizens Advice Bureau, or of your local welfare rights or advocacy service to find out about appeals procedures.

Eventually you should be allocated a care manager and a care plan. The plan should take account of all your needs: personal care, housing, independent living skills, travel and equipment. The social services and housing departments should work with your local health authority to meet your needs.

i	British Council of Disabled People (BCODP). Tel: 01332 295551, www.bcodp.org.uk.

British Council of Disabled People (BCODP). Tel: 01332 295551, www.bcodp.org.uk.

Carers National Association. Tel: 0345 573369 or 020 7490 8818.

Citizens Advice Bureau – see your local telephone directory for details.

National Centre for Independent Living. Tel: 020 7587 1663, www.ncil.org.uk. For details of your local independent living centre.

RADAR. Tel: 020 7250 3222, www.radar.org.uk. Publishes the Directory for Disabled People.

After my son was diagnosed I held on to the somewhat naïve notion that the problem would just disappear one day and that we would all live happily ever after.

At this stage it never occurred to me that it was in fact 'his' problem after all, surely I had earned ownership of it? I also had to face the fact that my efforts had served my needs to a much greater extent than the interests of my son. It was time to hand over the reins and take a supportive, rather than a leading role.

I had worked through anger and frustration with an education system and the ignorant, judgemental majority who never understood. From this came a final acceptance of the impossibility of doing this on someone else's behalf and protecting them from the pain. However tough the going was, I knew that he needed the space to learn the skills of everyday living and how to deal with authority and society at large on a day-to-day basis.

Letting go offered hope and opportunity as well as disappointment and worry. The alternative could have resulted in a life unfulfilled and an uneasy relationship of dependency. I have no regrets.

Cathy

ASSESSMENT FOR ADULTS WITH DEVELOPMENTAL DYSPRAXIA

There are many types of assessment that can be used on adults with dyspraxia – none of them specifically designed for them. Some of the assessments can only be done by psychologists or occupational therapists. Most, however, can be carried out by teachers, careers advisers, counsellors, etc. For more information on all the tests go to the relevant website. DANDA also has an adult dyspraxia checklist.

Adult Sensory Profile – Harcourt Assessment, www.harcourt-uk.com. Available to all.

AMPS: The Assessment of Motor and Process Skills – www.amps-uk.com. Accredited use required. Available to occupational therapists.

Behavioural Assessment of the Dysexecutive Syndrome (BADS) – Thames Valley Test Company, www.tvtc.com. Available to psychologists and occupational therapists.

Crawfords Small Part Dexterity Test – The Psychological Corporation, www.harcourt-uk.com. Available to all.

Fine Dexterity Test – www.morrisby.com. Available to all.

Gardner's Test of Visual Motor Skills (12–40) (TMVS-UL) – Ann Arbor Publishers, www.annarbor.co.uk.

Gardner's Test of Visual Perception Skills (Non Motor) Upper Level Revised (TVPS-UL-R) – Ann Arbor Publishers, www.annarbor.co.uk.

Grooved Peg Board Test – www.morrisby.com. Available to all.

Wechsler Adult Intelligence Scale 3rd Edition (WAIS 3) – Harcourt Assessment, www.harcourt-uk.com. Available only to psychologists.

Wide Range Achievement Test 3 (WRAT3) – Harcourt Assessment, www.harcourt-uk.com. Available to all.

Wide Range Intelligence Test 3 (WRIT3) – www.parinc.com. Available to all.

Appendix 4

INTERNATIONAL DYSPRAXIA CENTRES

AQED (Association Québécoise pour les Enfants Dyspraxique) – Canada
Contact: Sylvie Breton
212 7th Avenue South, Sherbrooke Quebec, Canada, J1G 2M7
Email: sylvie2223@sympatico.ca

Dyspraxia Association of Ireland
69a Main Street
Leixlip
Co. Kildare, Ireland
E-mail: info@dyspraxiaireland.com
www.dyspraxiaireland.com

Dyspraxia Centre – New Zealand
Contact: Mrs J. Davies
PO Box 20292
Bishopdale, Christchurch
New Zealand
E-mail: praxisnz@xtra.co.nz
www.dyspraxia.org.nz

Dyspraxia USA
120 S. Riverside Plaza
Chicago, IL 60606
United States
Tel: 001 312–207–0000.
www.dyspraxiausa.com – Mainly for adults.

ADULT DEVELOPMENTAL DYSPRAXIA (DCD) QUESTIONNAIRE

Introduciton

The purpose of this questionnaire is to serve as a screening tool for developmental dyspraxia in adulthood. Its aim is simply to give an indication of whether somebody might have developmental dyspraxia. It is not intended to replace a full diagnostic assessment by a qualified professional.

I have been asked by teachers, universities, employers, trade unions and dyspraxics themselves for such a checklist. It is based to some extent on existing checklists for adult dyslexia and dyspraxia, but is much more detailed. The questions are based on ten years of experience of working with adult dyspraxia and speaking to adult dyspraxics on the helpline and in person.

The great detail of this questionnaire means it is likely to provide a more accurate assessment. For example, it includes questions on medical or family history, as well as greater detail on specific difficulties. It also looks at the degree and frequency of difficulties, rather than just requesting yes/no responses.

The questionnaire is not normed in any way, but the author would like to encourage research on it so that it can be normed. While the questions focus very much on the negative aspects of dyspraxia, as is necessary in a screening test, it must be emphasised that there are many positive characteristics of dyspraxia, for example determination, caring, originality and good strategic thinking.

If you find that you have affiliation with several areas on the questionnaire you should consider seeking professional assessment.

The author would welcome any comments from people who have used the questionnaire.

Adult Developmental Dyspraxia (DCD) questionnaire

Please circle the appropriate answer for each question. Ideally, fill it in in the company of a professional.

Please note:

If you find that you have most of the symptoms mentioned in these questions, you should not assume that you definitely have developmental dyspraxia. However, it may be worth seeking a diagnosis or assessment from a relevant professional.

1. Personal history

Did you have difficulties at, or just after birth (e.g. early/difficult delivery, feeding problems)?

Severe   Moderate   Mild   None   Don't know

Did you have any difficulties in early infancy (e.g. late sitting, walking, talking)?

Severe   Moderate   Mild   None   Don't know

Did you crawl?

Yes   No

Any other details or comments about personal history:

2. Education

Did you have problems with schoolwork?

Severe   Moderate   Mild   None

Did you have particular problems with PE/sport?

Severe   Moderate   Mild   None

Were you bullied at school?

Often   Sometimes   Rarely   No

Did you truant from school?

Often   Sometimes   Rarely   No

Did you have problems interacting with other children at school?

Any other details or comments about education problems?

3. Employment

Are you (or have you ever been) employed? Yes   No

If 'Yes', please answer the following four questions.
If 'No' please go to Question 4.

Did you find it hard to choose a career?

Very hard   Hard   Slightly hard   No

Did you find it harder to get a job than the average person?

Much harder   Harder   Slightly harder   No

Did you find it harder than most to keep a job?

Much harder   Harder   Slightly harder   No

Have you experienced difficulties in the workplace?

Very often   Quite often   Sometimes   Never

Any other details/comments about employment problems?

4. Medical history

Did you have problems with hearing, when you were a child (e.g. glue ear)?

Severe   Moderate   Mild   None   Don't know

Do you have any allergies?

Severe   Moderate   Mild   None   Don't know

Do you have any aches and pains in your joints?

Severe   Moderate   Mild   None

Do you have any food intolerances?

Severe   Moderate   Mild   None   Don't know

Do you have asthma or eczema?

Severe   Moderate   Mild   No

Do you have irritable bowel syndrome?

Severe   Moderate   Mild   No   Don't know

Do you have epilepsy?

Severe   Moderate   Mild   No

Do you have diabetes?

Severe   Moderate   Mild   No   Don't know

Do you have any other specific learning disabilities (SpLD)
e.g. dyslexia, ADD, Asperger's Syndrome?

Yes   No   Perhaps   Don't know

Does any member of your family have an SpLD such as
dyspraxia, dyslexia, co-ordination problems, ADD or
Asperger's Syndrome?

Yes   No   Perhaps   Don't know

If yes, please state which.

5. Co-ordination (gross motor activities)

Do you have poor posture?

Yes   No

Do you find it difficult to stand for a long time (e.g. because
of poor muscle tone or balance)?

Very difficult   Difficult   Not difficult

Do you bump into things or people and often trip over, e.g. because of lack of awareness in space?

Very often   Often   Rarely   Rarely   No

Do you find it difficult walking up and downhills or down the stairs?

Very difficult   Difficult   A bit difficult   Not difficult   No

Do you find sports difficult?

Very difficult	Difficult	A bit difficult	Not difficult	Can't do it at all	Never tried

Team games

Very difficult	Difficult	A bit difficult	Not difficult	Can't do it at all	Never tried

Bat and ball games

Very difficult	Difficult	A bit difficult	Not difficult	Can't do it at all	Never tried

Aerobics

Very difficult	Difficult	A bit difficult	Not difficult	Can't do it at all	Never tried

Keep fit exercises

Very difficult	Difficult	A bit difficult	Not difficult	Can't do it at all	Never tried

Riding a bike

Very difficult	Difficult	A bit difficult	Not difficult	Can't do it at all	Never tried

Dancing

| Very difficult | Difficult | A bit difficult | Not difficult | Can't do it at all | Never tried |

Gym

| Very difficult | Difficult | A bit difficult | Not difficult | Can't do it at all | Never tried |

6. Co-ordination (fine motor activities)

Do you find it difficult to do practical or fine motor tasks such as:

Domestic chores

| Very difficult | Difficult | A bit difficult | Not difficult | Can't do it at all | Never tried |

Cooking, e.g. measuring things, cutting, peeling, pouring

| Very difficult | Difficult | A bit difficult | Not difficult | Can't do it at all | Never tried |

DIY

| Very difficult | Difficult | A bit difficult | Not difficult | Can't do it at all | Never tried |

Typing

| Very difficult | Difficult | A bit difficult | Not difficult | Can't do it at all | Never tried |

Driving a car

| Very difficult | Difficult | A bit difficult | Not difficult | Can't do it at all | Never tried |

Operating machinery

| Very difficult | Difficult | A bit difficult | Not difficult | Can't do it at all | Never tried |

Craftwork/sewing

| Very difficult | Difficult | A bit difficult | Not difficult | Can't do it at all | Never tried |

Working on a computer

| Very difficult | Difficult | A bit difficult | Not difficult | Can't do it at all | Never tried |

Playing a musical instrument

| Very difficult | Difficult | A bit difficult | Not difficult | Can't do it at all | Never tried |

Drawing diagrams or shapes etc.

| Very difficult | Difficult | A bit difficult | Not difficult | Can't do it at all | Never tried |

Using locks and keys

| Very difficult | Difficult | A bit difficult | Not difficult | Can't do it at all | Never tried |

Do you find it difficult to manage your personal care?

Shaving

| Very difficult | Difficult | A bit difficult | Not difficult | Not applicable |

Make-up, e.g. applying mascara

| Very difficult | Difficult | A bit difficult | Not difficult | Not applicable |

Clothes, e.g. zips, fasteners, shoe-laces

Very difficult	Difficult	A bit difficult	Not difficult	Not applicable

Washing

Very difficult	Difficult	A bit difficult	Not difficult	Not applicable

Do you spill and drop things more often than others?

Much more often	More often	A bit more often	No

7. Orientation/perception

Do you find it difficult:

...to find your way in a strange place?

Very difficult	Difficult	A bit difficult	Not difficult

...to follow left or right instructions?

Very difficult	Difficult	A bit difficult	Not difficult

...to tell the time on the clock face?

Very difficult	Difficult	A bit difficult	Not difficult

...to read a map?

Very difficult	Difficult	A bit difficult	Not difficult

...to judge a distance and space?

Very difficult	Difficult	A bit difficult	Not difficult

...to follow a time-table?

Very difficult	Difficult	A bit difficult	Not difficult

...to look things up in a dictionary or telephone directory?

Very difficult   Difficult   A bit difficult   Not difficult

Are you over-sensitive to:
...sound, e.g. working against background noise?

Very over-sensitive   Over-sensitive   A bit over-sensitive   No

...touch, e.g. texture of some materials?

Very over-sensitive   Over-sensitive   A bit over-sensitive   No

...smell, e.g. cooking smells, smoke?

Very over-sensitive   Over-sensitive   A bit over-sensitive   No

...temperature?

Very over-sensitive   Over-sensitive   A bit over-sensitive   No

Are you under-sensitive to:
...sound, e.g. working against background noise?

Very under-sensitive   Under-sensitive   A bit under-sensitive   No

...touch, e.g. texture of some materials?

Very under-sensitive   Under-sensitive   A bit under-sensitive   No

...smell, e.g. cooking smells, smoke?

Very under-sensitive   Under-sensitive   A bit under-sensitive   No

...temperature?

Very under-sensitive   Under-sensitive   A bit under-sensitive   No

8. Concentration, memory and organisation
Are you generally disorganised and untidy?

Very disorganised   Disorganised   A bit   No

Do you find it harder than most to maintain focus and concentration?

Very hard   Hard   A bit hard   Rarely

Do you sometimes over-compensate for your lack of organisation, e.g. obsessively writing out endless lists?

Yes   Sometimes   No

Do you find it hard to remember and follow instructions?

Very hard   Hard   A bit hard   Rarely

Do you find it hard to do mental arithmetic?

Very hard   Hard   A bit hard   Rarely

Do you find it hard to concentrate for long periods?

Very hard   Hard   A bit hard   Rarely

Do you find it hard to take messages and pass them on correctly?

Very hard   Hard   A bit hard   Rarely

Do you find it hard to dial the correct numbers on the phone?

Very hard   Hard   A bit hard   Rarely

Do you tend to over-focus on a particular project?

Very often   Quite often   Sometimes   Rarely

Do you mix up dates and times and miss appointments?

Very often   Quite often   Sometimes   Rarely

Do you lose things often and find it difficult to remember where you have put them?

Very often   Quite often   Sometimes   Rarely

Do you find it hard to do more than one thing at a time?

Very hard   Hard   A bit hard   Rarely

Do you have problems prioritising and discriminating the essential from the inessential?

Very often   Quite often   Sometimes   Rarely

Do you operate in a muddled way generally?

Very often   Quite often   Sometimes   Rarely

Do you have difficulties shopping, remembering what you wanted to buy?

Very difficult   Difficult   A bit difficult   Rarely

Do you have difficulty calculating the change?

Very difficult   Difficult   A bit difficult   Rarely

Do you forget to pay bills?

Very often   Often   Sometimes   Rarely

Do you have difficulty managing your finances?

Very difficult   Difficult   A bit difficult   Rarely

9. Speech, listening and comprehension (including social interaction)

Do you find it difficult to explain things to people simply and clearly?

Very difficult   Difficult   A bit difficult   Rarely

Do you go off on tangents?

Very often   Often   Sometimes   Rarely

Do people find it hard to understand what you say?

Very often   Often   Sometimes   Rarely

Are you often misunderstood?

Very often   Often   Sometimes   Rarely

When you say a long word, do you sometimes find it difficult to get sounds in the right order?

Very often   Often   Sometimes   Rarely

Do you sometimes talk too loudly/softly or slowly/quickly?

Very often   Often   Sometimes   Rarely

Please give details:

Do you 'lose the thread' of conversation or discussions because you're day-dreaming?

Very often   Often   Sometimes   Rarely

Do you find group discussion or conversation especially difficult?

Very often   Often   Sometimes   Rarely

Do you sometimes blank out when engaged in discussion?

Very often   Often   Sometimes   Rarely

Do you find it difficult to take notes at a lecture or meeting?

Very difficult   Difficult   A bit difficult   Never

Is there a delay between hearing something and understanding it?

Very often   Often   Sometimes   Rarely

Do you take spoken and written words literally and find it hard to understand nuances?

Very often   Often   Sometimes   Rarely

Do you find it difficult to interpret body language?

Very difficult   Difficult   A bit difficult   Never

Do you interrupt people, e.g. because of your impulsivity and/or short-term memory problems)?

Very often   Often   Sometimes   Rarely

Do you find it difficult to make friends and keep them?

Very difficult   Difficult   A bit difficult   Never

Do you find it hard to be consistent and have 'good' and 'bad' days?

Very often   Often   Sometimes   Rarely

10. Writing

Is your handwriting untidy and difficult to read?

Very often   Often   Sometimes   Rarely

Is your spelling poor especially when under stress?

Very poor   Poor   A bit poor   No

Do you put letters and numbers in the wrong order?

Very often   Often   Sometimes   Rarely

Do you find it difficult putting your ideas down on paper?

Very difficult   Difficult   A bit difficult   Rarely

Do you find it difficult to fill in forms?

Very difficult   Difficult   A bit difficult   Rarely

Do you have difficulties writing a cheque?

Very difficult   Difficult   A bit difficult   Rarely

Do you have problems with organising and writing a report/ essay?

Very difficult   Difficult   A bit difficult   Rarely

Do you have problems proofreading?

Very difficult   Difficult   A bit difficult   Rarely

Do you have difficulties finishing off a piece of work?

Very difficult   Difficult   A bit difficult   Rarely

11. Reading

Do you find it hard to remember what you have read?

Very hard   Hard   A bit hard   Rarely

Do you lose your place when you are reading?

Very often   Often   Sometimes   Rarely

Do words on a page seen to 'jump about'?

Very often   Often   Sometimes   Rarely   Never

Do you find it difficult to follow a plot or sequence of events?

Very difficult   Difficult   A bit difficult   Rarely

12. Your reactions to your difficulties

Please circle any of the following words or phases which you feel
describe your reaction to your difficulties:

frustrated	angry	confused	low self-esteem
phobic	defensive	aggressive	low confidence
irritable	anxious	passive	misunderstood
stressed	depressed	guilty	disempowered
fatigued	embarrassed		

13. Any other comments

THE MAKE-UP OF NEURO-DIVERSITY

This is a document for discussion, concentrating mainly on the difficulties of those with deuro-diversity. It must, however, be pointed out that many people with neuto-diversity are excellent at maths, co-ordination, reading etc. We are people of extremes.

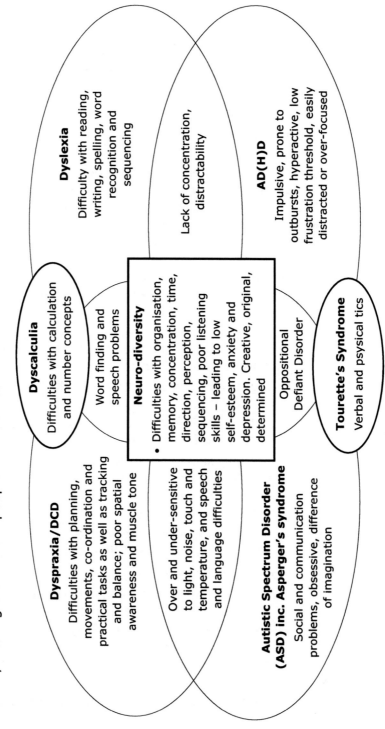

Dyslexia
Difficulty with reading, writing, spelling, word recognition and sequencing

Lack of concentration, distractability

AD(H)D
Impulsive, prone to outbursts, hyperactive, low frustration threshold, easily distracted or over-focused

Dyscalculia
Difficulties with calculation and number concepts

Word finding and speech problems

Neuro-diversity
• Difficulties with organisation, memory, concentration, time, direction, perception, sequencing, poor listening skills – leading to low self-esteem, anxiety and depression. Creative, original, determined

Oppositional Defiant Disorder

Tourette's Syndrome
Verbal and psysical tics

Dyspraxia/DCD
Difficulties with planning, movements, co-ordination and practical tasks as well as tracking and balance; poor spatial awareness and muscle tone

Over and under-sensitive to light, noise, touch and temperature, and speech and language difficulties

Autistic Spectrum Disorder (ASD) inc. Asperger's syndrome
Social and communication problems, obsessive, difference of imagination

DANDA: DEVELOPMENTAL ADULT NEURO-DIVERSITY ASSOCIATION

danda NETWORK

The Newsletter of the Developmental Adult Neuro-diversity Association

DANDA, a registered charity, provides support and assistance for people with neuro-diversity after they have left school. Neuro-diversity includes conditions such as dyspraxia, dyslexia, attention deficit disorder and Asperger's syndrome. It focuses particularly on conditions that are relatively little understood, e.g. dyspraxia.

The scope of the Group includes:

- raising awareness of dyspraxia and related conditions which affect adults
- offering support, advice and information to adults with dyspraxia and related conditions and professionals who work with them
- organising conferences on adult dyspraxia and related conditions
- aiming to simplify and increase diagnosis of dyspraxia and related conditions
- running a network of local contacts (some local groups run social and self-help groups)
- publication of newsletter *DANDA Network* twice each year
- representation at conferences and exhibitions for adults with dyspraxic difficulties.

Recent activities include:

- a lively e-mailing list with nearly 500 members which is associated with the Group
- close collaboration with the Disability Rights Commission, who are setting up a Neuro-diversity/Autistic Spectrum Disorder Action Group
- publications, including *Dyspraxic Voices*.

For details of the Group, contact:

Mary Colley
Tel: 020 7435 7891
E-mail: mary.colley@danda.org.uk
Website: www.danda.org.uk

To join the e-mailing list for adult dyspraxics visit:
dyspraxia-subscribe@yahoogroups.com

INDEX